Tales from the Wishbone Tree

A story of love, loss and survival

Tales from the Wishbone Tree

A story of love, loss and survival

Helly Eaton

BOOKS

Winchester, UK
Washington, USA

First published by O-Books, 2019
O-Books is an imprint of John Hunt Publishing Ltd., 3 East St., Alresford,
Hampshire SO24 9EE, UK
office1@jhpbooks.net
www.johnhuntpublishing.com
www.o-books.com

For distributor details and how to order please visit the 'Ordering' section on our website.

Text copyright: Helly Eaton 2018

ISBN: 978 1 78904 119 4
978 1 78904 120 0 (ebook)
Library of Congress Control Number: 2018941727

A CIP catalogue record for this book is available from the British Library.

Design: Stuart Davies

UK: Printed and bound by CPI Group (UK) Ltd, Croydon, CR0 4YY
US: Printed and bound by Thomson Shore, 7300 West Joy Road, Dexter, MI 48130

We operate a distinctive and ethical publishing philosophy in
all areas of our business, from our global network of authors to
production and worldwide distribution.

Contents

A Word Before We Start...

When I first wrote this, I wasn't intending for you to read it. It was more for me than for you. It was good to get it out of my system, to try to make some sense of it all. After a while, I guess the old journo habits kicked in and I started to arrange it into sections. Before, during, after, now – then?

Now it's an open book in more ways than one. Read it all or dip in and out, it's up to you. You may want to skip the diary bit completely (I wish I could've, too) and pick about in the rest. Or whatever – your choice.

Just be assured it's all real. I've been moved and directed to write it as it is.

So many of us go through these things when we lose someone we love and there are lots of 'guides' and 'words of wisdom' out there. But we're all different and even when going through similar experiences, react and respond in our own individual ways.

So this isn't a guide, it's just how it happened for me. And since none of us is going to get out of here alive, it will eventually affect us all...

Tales From the Wishbone Tree

Part One

Views From the Edge

It was spring 2015. And until then I was pretty normal.

It all started simply enough and in many ways was the usual story. My husband Robin and I had moved down to Dorset from Sussex the year before, heading west like so many before us. We'd been married 10 years – still happy we'd found a late but wildly flowering relationship that continually surprised us. We soon discovered some like-hearted, light-minded friends in our village. Even our quirky cats and rescue dog bounced into their new 'escape to the country'. It was all to play for – new environment, new haunts to eat and drink, new friends, new adventures. We were the envy of friends and family.

But then life threw us a curveball. At first, I wrote about it a day at a time. It was the only way to handle it then, bit by bit...

10 April 2015

After suffering months of discomfort and pain beneath his ribcage on his left side, Robin finally convinced his new GP to refer him for an endoscopy. This was The Day. He was hoping he'd at last discover what was actually wrong with him instead of enduring endless guesswork from the doctors and locums he had seen at the GP practice. He'd had endoscopies in the past so wasn't unduly worried about the procedure. We weren't expecting what happened next.

They called me in from the waiting room and I found Robin in a side room, pale and quiet. The nurse said simply that the endoscopy had shown a substantial growth in the oesophagus and the clinical nurse specialist would come down shortly to go through it all with us. By then we were both 'pale and quiet', surprised and in shock.

Specialist nurse Jane arrived. I had a mass of questions and Jane was lovely, calm and kind. It wasn't long before the C word came up. They'd taken a biopsy which would confirm whether the growth was malignant. There would also be a CT scan and an appointment with the consultant after that to go through the final diagnosis and options. Jane looked as though she already knew where all this was going and my questions were being gently guided down the 'probability of cancer' route. But the consultant would review all the results and go through it with us after the scan.

The CT scan was arranged for 10 days' time. (10 whole days?! What were we supposed to do in the meantime? Wasn't speed vital with potentially life-threatening diagnoses?) But it was out of our hands – we were now 'in the system'. It was both a relief that someone was taking him seriously at last, and also the scariest thing in the world.

We left the hospital dazed and conflicted. Robin was satisfied, in a way, that there had been something wrong all along and that he wasn't 'malingering' at the GP's. And once we knew exactly what it was, we could do something about it. We hoped.

We had a hassled week of restless sleep. It was hard not to overthink it, and were buoying each other up to get through the uncertain days. We told some of our close people, but not everyone yet as there was no really definite news or plans for treatment until after the scan.

Robin was in pain and discomfort following the endoscopy and biopsy, and wasn't eating much. I made loads of soups and smoothies, and tried to keep active and positive.

We somehow got through the days. When the sun came out we spent a bright afternoon down at West Bay with an excited Freya dog barking and playing in the sea. It was good and very therapeutic. The next day we walked along the local stream, enjoying the simple pleasures of wood anemones and tiny new lambs.

The cherry tree in the front garden just outside my window was bursting with buds, obliviously pushing forward into spring. The garden, after Robin's earlier hard work and totally unaware of the turmoil inside the house, was bursting out all over and already looking lovely. And Robin had plans for much, much more.

21 April 2015

The CT scan was pretty straightforward and a familiar procedure. It wasn't the first time we'd been in this department. Unfortunately the previous scan and ultrasound they did on Robin was apparently 'abdomen only' and didn't include the now all-important upper digestive tract. ('Why???' I wanted to scream.) No news yet. The consultant appointment was the following day.

22 April 2015

Okay this was it. We drove the 30 miles to Weymouth hospital to see the consultant. When we went in, he started with the words, 'This is bad news I'm afraid.' He actually looked afraid. He told us the cancer was at the base of the oesophagus and top of stomach, and had also spread to a small spot on the liver. It was inoperable. He said Robin had months rather than years.

Robin was amazingly calm and asked lots of questions. As I sat there listening to one bad thing after another, my mind dissolved and I fainted. I'm not usually the fainting kind, and when I came to, the consultant and nurse were kneeling beside me asking if I was all right. Dumb question...

Unfortunately, because I'd had pulmonary embolisms three months before, they were telling me to go back to Dorchester hospital and get checked out. The timing couldn't have been worse. With Robin's blindingly bleak diagnosis, the last place we wanted to go was another hospital. He drove me there and although was obviously struggling with being back at Dorchester, he was still kindness itself in spite of his far greater problems and obvious shock. We left after a couple of hours and headed home.

By then we were both feeling sick, cold and shattered. It was the most awful day. We laid low and decided to tell people tomorrow, though we did both call our sisters in the end.

We had a fitful night, waking and dozing in turns, holding each other, feeling devastated. Terms like 'sick with worry' and 'frozen with fear' suddenly made perfect sense to me, obviously coined by those feeling as we did now.

23 April 2015

We felt a bit easier on waking, not quite so panicky or sick. We phoned and emailed all our main people. The hardest bit was hearing their shock and devastation, not to mention tears and outrage.

We went shopping to get some easy things for Robin to eat – veggies for soups and smoothies. Wine for me. We were trying to be normal. Feeling anything but.

Later we took Freya to Charmouth beach – I was trying hard not to think how many more times we'd come here. Dorset countryside is so rapturously beautiful in the sunshine. How could I ever enjoy being here without Robin?

He made Thai noodle soup for supper and we both ate some. It was gorgeous and light. He decided he would go off to his short mat bowls club at the Village Hall this evening. I was glad he felt normal enough to do that. Me, I was reading lots of heartfelt replies to our earlier emails. And writing this.

24–27 April 2015

Up, down, up, down. Days of trying to do normal things like shopping, walking Freya, talking to people etc. Not feeling normal. It was a very grey day on Sunday and Robin wasn't well. We pushed ourselves to go to an Open Garden nearby that was supposed to be ravishing and it truly was. Sadly we weren't.

28 April 2015

We had an early appointment at Dorchester hospital to see the senior oncology consultant. We were both, we realised later, dreading it – imagining more of last week's gloom and doom. I had been busy online researching various new cancer treatment trials Robin could possibly go on and felt I had weapons in my armoury ready for firing. Actually I felt more like a wet dishcloth.

BUT it was good news, or what passed as good news to us those days. Yes, he said, Robin was a prime candidate for the gold standard drug cocktail chemotherapy cycle to hopefully halt but also (I *heard* him say it) to *shrink* the tumours.

No promises obviously. But he mentioned the '3 months', '6 months', '9 months', 'next year' words that were sheer music to my ears. The drugs may or may not work, he said, but the side effects were usually tolerable and if not they could consider a different mix.

Suddenly, there were options. There were possibilities. I was joyful. There may be no cures, but there were more chances than there were yesterday.

Robin has been brilliant. But when we left he was quiet and obviously worried. Having felt so ill and awful over the past few months, he was now imagining this heavy new regime might actually make him feel even worse and admitted he's not good with pain and discomfort. This from the man who'd had endoscopies and colonoscopies, tests, scans and other procedures with aplomb. But he was so tired from going through all this for so long, the hurtling juggernaut of toxic medicines and hospital visits heading his way seemed to be painting a pretty grim future. It was the unknown again. And who could blame him.

He managed to eat a good meal and went to bed early. It's another day tomorrow. My joy was tempered with a heavy dose of reality. But it was still better than yesterday. For me anyway.*[1]

29 April 2015

Another hiccup. Robin had toothache and the info about chemo from the hospital said to get all this checked out before chemo starts. So he saw the dentist first thing today and apparently had a gum infection and needed two teeth out. After phoning Jane, our clinical specialist nurse, he tried to get an early appointment to have the teeth extracted asap. The chemo would have to be postponed.

After the initial relief that some sort of treatment was about to start at the hospital after all this time, this frustration, at least for me, was mind grabbing. The chemo department said to come for the pre-chemo appointment today anyway so we spent the afternoon at the hospital. Chemo nurse Caroline talked us through the whole thing and super-efficiently sorted everything on the phone with Robin's dentist as though she did all this sort of thing all the time. She does, of course. And she did it so well. The chemo itself was pushed back just a week, and in the meantime, poor Robin had a dental appointment the next morning to have the teeth extracted, followed by a week on antibiotics to clear any infection. Sigh. Phew. It's never up but it's down.

I hoped perhaps the extra week would give him time to get used to the chemo idea and calm his spirit. It's been so tough for him.

All the emails and phone calls from family and friends were lovely, positive and bright. Everyone was rooting for him. Me too. In buckets.

30 April 2015

Not a good start. Robin woke up in pain thinking this may now be the norm. He went to the dentist anyway and had the two teeth out, but they wouldn't give him the required antibiotics the chemo nurse had asked for. Back home again we got on the phone to the chemo dept and they were wonderful, instantly reassuring, and organised the medication direct with our doctor.

We did some shopping and then went to the GP's to pick up the antibiotics as well as Robin's new protein drinks to help him get enough nutrients when he couldn't eat properly. A huge crate full of bottles appeared in reception. Robin at least managed a smile, saying they obviously thought he'd be around for a while yet to give him so many...

I made risotto for supper – a disaster as he couldn't eat it. So keen was I to find something light and tasty, I'd completely forgotten the 'not being able to chew because of having had teeth out' situation. It all landed up in the bin. What am I like. It served me right. I felt awful.

The evening picked up with us watching *The Good Wife* on TV in bed. Peace and harmony was restored. What would tomorrow bring?

1–2 May 2015

Starting the day on a positive note, we dug out Robin's ancient blender from the back of the cupboard (more used to mixing cocktails in his wild youth) and started whizzing up some carrot and tangerine juice. It got very thick and pulpy so I went online for some suggestions. Aha! Squeeze it out in a muslin bag or similar, said a woman on YouTube – the pith stays in bag and a lovely smooth juice emerges. I used our Onya net vegetable bags and got perfect results – it even tasted great.

Spurred on, I chopped some veggies for soup and got the breadmaker going. Domestic goddess? Hardly, but it felt better to be doing something useful. Then I made lemon and coriander pasta for supper which was yum and easy to eat (I hoped), but Robin gave up halfway through and fancied cereal and yogurt instead. He was taking his herbal tonic*2 twice a day now, so I must brew some more in a couple of days.

By then he decided it was time for his sister Lynne to come down (she'd been wanting to for ages but had been selflessly giving him space to adjust and adapt to the big C news) so I arranged for that, too. I reckoned it'd be very emotional but also good for them both, and for me. I went into mad cleaning and washing for tomorrow. (It's known locally here as 'immaculating' your house for visitors...)

I gave Robin a massage this afternoon. He was obviously very tense and anxious, quite naturally given what was going on, but responded brilliantly and relaxed enough to watch a Nick Cave documentary, sipping his protein drink.

Everyone round here was so thoughtful and kind. Quite humbling. And also very nurturing for us both.

3 May 2015

We had a bad night with one of our elderly cats keeping us both awake. R got very stressed, me I was just knackered. In the morning, Robin asked me to call Lynne and suggest we abandon today for her visit as he said he just wasn't up to seeing anyone.

It would be good to wake up from this nightmare. The weather was rainy and windy (typical bank holiday) and perfectly mirrored our spirits. I took Freya dog out – walking in the fields is always very therapeutic, even in the rain. But when I got back I found Robin slumped on the bed feeling so ill he thought he was dying. He'd been hoovering the house and then mowed the grass and had obviously overdone it. We talked, I listened and encouraged. He then agreed to try a healing meditation tape that a friend had given us. It relaxed him down and I tempted him afterwards with juices and soup.

It's pretty hard all this and it amazed me that so many people go through these things every day and still carry on. I was doing my best to be positive and support Robin, but it was knackering emotionally and physically for both of us, and we'd barely started yet. I thought perhaps you might slip into a rhythm when the chemo treatment starts. I hoped so.

4 May 2015

What a difference a day makes. After a good night's sleep Robin was feeling much better. His sister Lynne and brother-in-law Philip arrived at 11ish and after a few emotional hugs and hellos, we had a splendid, mostly normal spring day, walking in the bluebell woods, having Indonesian noodle soup for lunch followed by tea and biscuits, even laughs and jokes around the table. It was heaven and so lovely to see and hear Robin being positive and happy. A joyful day.

6 May 2015

Yesterday Robin went for his dental deep clean – poor guy, it seemed to be coming all at once for him. His face was frozen for most of the day from numerous injections, so he was unable to eat, drink or even sip. He bore it bravely, though, and we gorged on *Game of Thrones* episodes...

Today was more positive again. I noticed a slight gallows humour coming in now which was a little disconcerting at first. He was also going through his watch collection and sending off special ones to his sister and nieces, and organising others for his special friends. He said he was just saying in the cards that he's 'still here, don't worry', but I was sure they would. It was a lovely thought but perhaps a bit premature. Or not. Who knows.

We went to Bridport to buy a hat for when his hair falls out from chemo – we laughed as he looked like a groovy rock god. Well, I suppose he was really. I bought some new specs. He was going to, too, but joked about whether it was worth it. (There was that gallows humour again.) New phone or not new phone? Monthly tariff or just a new sim card till 'whenever' ... It was a bit hard to deal with this new jokey stuff. Or maybe it wasn't jokey at all. That was the terrifying bit.

8 May 2015

Here we go. Chemo day. We had an early start for Robin's

first session at DCH (Dorchester County Hospital). Our lovely neighbour Mel was helping us out with dog walking, even though she'd had a late night herself after election duties in Bridport until the early hours.

The chemo department was empty when we arrived at the prescribed 8.30am, and we waited a while before seeing the chemo nurse. She smiled reassuringly but then took Robin briskly away for his treatment. No room for partners or friends in the chemo suite apparently and I suddenly felt bereft. Robin and I had been through so much of this together over the last few months, it seemed strange and cruel that they whisked him away to sit there around six hours on his own. When I asked, they said that the chemo area wasn't big enough for 'extra people'. I felt a like a spare part.

So I spent the morning instead walking round Dorchester wandering in and out of shops, barely noticing what I was seeing. The grey rainy weather reflected just how I felt. I'd wanted to be there for this hardest part with him as I know you can at other hospitals, but for now the medics in their wisdom thought that wasn't necessary. Hmm.

I found a 'potters' coffee shop with steaming, comforting hot chocolate and a toasted teacake big enough to feed four. I managed it to chomp my way through it, though, surprisingly easily as it happens.

Back at hospital the C department was now heaving with people coming and going. Robin eventually emerged in the corridor, looking very wobbly and wan. He'd been very sick and they'd given him extra anti-nausea injections. He looked as grey as I felt. After another while, they let him leave, loaded up with bags of medications: chemo tablets for 21 days, 3 lots of different anti-nausea pills, one lot of anti-constipation pills, one lot of anti-diarrhoea pills, plus steroids and ampoules to give to the district nurse to inject if the nausea persisted over the weekend.

He looked really terrible. And felt the same, it seemed. We had to stop on the way home as he was violently sick again. I wanted to wrap him up and hold him for ever, but getting home was the priority. He went straight to bed and slept. I gave him fluids and put an old bowl by the bed in case he needed it again. He slept more. I ironed. Lovely Mel walked a very confused Freya again. Thank god for brilliant neighbours and kind friends. Thank you.

The cherry blossom on the tree outside the window as I write this is swaying gorgeously in the wind and rain. Beautiful and courageous in spite of the wet withering weather. I guess there's a lesson in there somewhere but I was too tired to see it just then.

10 May 2015

Days like yesterday are best forgotten though they can't be, I suppose, because they're all part of the same story. Robin's sickness and weakness became all-pervading and he wasn't able even to get out of bed. He was in the sort of pain and discomfort that made him (and me) wonder if it was all worth it. Was this juggernaut of drugs blindly careering through his system really the best way forward? I would have given anything to take the strain and pain from him, but instead, was only able to love and support, reassure and nurture him through this awful journey.

Night-time was the worst. He couldn't get comfortable and the area of the tumour itself was tight and painful. He seemed to consider that dying might be the healthiest option. I massaged his hands and feet, brought him a hot water bottle, offered him lavender and paracetamol, and gave him healing. Morning came eventually and I could hear him gently snoring. The relief was palpable as he was at last comfortable and resting peacefully.

Today has been better in its way. Still some nausea and discomfort, but he seemed a bit brighter in spirit. I took Freya out for a long therapeutic walk (for both of us) across the fields, down to the stream and round the village. When I got back, Robin was sitting downstairs, dressed and with colour in his cheeks. He wasn't able to eat yet but was at least drinking fluids and was persuaded to try some fruit for lunch. Melon and banana were about the only things that he could get down at the moment. The protein shakes were off the radar because they're milky and he couldn't bear the thought. I phoned to see if the GP could get us the juice-based ones instead.

Various people phoned and texted but I was just too knackered to talk to many of them. I decided to send a joint email like a 'bulletin from the palace' and hoped they understood for the moment. Family excepted, of course. It's always good to hear your nearest and dearest down the phone. But there wasn't much I could say at the moment. Being a glass half full kind of person, this continuous gloom was especially hard to report on. I kept looking for the light at the end of the tunnel. There's been a tiny bit of light today and I just hoped it wasn't an oncoming train...

11 May 2015

We slept well, which is good. For me anyway. Robin wasn't so good in the morning and was wide awake when I woke up, uncomfortable and restless. I made him some tea but his stomach was tight and he was shaking. I held him close and after a while did some breathing exercises with him. Hand massage helped calm things down a bit.

Later in the morning, he actually felt better and got up. By the time I was back from my walk with Freya, he was sitting downstairs in the lounge, which was great.

My walk was lovely – it's hard to beat sun and spring fields, a magic combination. Except Freya got zapped by an electric fence and bolted for home and her dad. I managed to catch up with her and calm her down a bit, but there was only one person she needed to comfort her and it wasn't me. Robin made a big fuss of her when we got home and she was soon fine.

He was listening to Radio 4 and someone had apparently mentioned ham and egg. It got him thinking and he fancied giving it a go. I had to nip out anyway to get some supplies, so ham was top of my agenda. Success! It's amazing that it only takes one slice of honey roast ham and one egg to totally make our day. Yay!

He walked round the garden, his personal paradise, and pottered happily for a while. I could feel that his spirit was back. He had colour in his face, he made a few jokes, smiled a few smiles and then came in to loaf on the sofa, content just for a while.

But fatigue catches up pretty fast and soon he retreated again upstairs. We're trying acupressure wrist bands to help with the nausea (the kind you wear for travel sickness). And I've got the new protein juices instead of shakes from the doctor so they don't taste so milky and yuk. All good.

The small moments of 'normality' helped us cope with the many times that were anything but. And there were more normal bits each day. The hospital called today to see how he's doing and if he's all right. They couldn't have been nicer and said he'd soon be having chips with his ham and eggs. Ha ha. Big joke.

(But fingers crossed…)

13 May 2015

Yesterday was a good day. Robin's spirit was back and he ate real food, albeit in small amounts. He came for a walk with Freya and me, just round the village but it's great to see him out. He went online and ordered a new TV and a hover mower.

It started well today, too. Then quickly fatigue set in. He chatted with me about how things have changed for him and how this is such a huge learning curve. He's having to listen to exactly what his body tells him now and pace himself instead of hurtling headlong into doing things as before. He said he's noticing the small things so much more and that even in the darkest moments there are sometimes the tiniest flashes of joy – too quick to hang on to but enough just to notice. The birds singing outside the window, the rich silence of the countryside around us, the dog or the cat on the bed, the momentary smell or taste of something exquisite.

But then the nausea or tiredness kick in again. His lucidity and understanding humble me. I'm trying to do everything he normally does, trying to find him things he'll want and be able to eat, second guessing how he's going to be, hoping and praying he'll respond well and not give up.

His joy gave me joy. His normality made life fine for the moment. We were very much living in the now, as they say. I'd always wanted to do that. But not this way or for this reason. It's a shame that it took such a sledgehammer to knock that simple lesson into my simple brain.

Later I walked through the fields with the dog, completely at one with my surroundings, loving living here. But the deep ache continued to gnaw away inside and I longed to wake up from this nightmare and embrace normality with my new, enlightened passion.

I hoped there'd be another good day. And another. And another. But taking one day at a time was all we could do at the moment. People round here were incredibly kind and supportive. They weren't flooding us, but we knew beyond a shadow of a doubt they were solidly there if we needed them. As some had their own problems too, there was a strong feeling that we're all in this together helping each other through. It's a good village and we're very lucky.

18 May 2015

After a couple of terrible days with Robin feeling weak and ill and staying in bed, we suddenly seemed to have turned a corner. It was 10 days after the first chemo session and he was up and about for two days and eating well, albeit little and often. He'd lost loads of weight but was now actually thinking and talking about food, what he fancied and what he could eat. I'd been juicing with my new Lidl bright pink cheerful juicer and it had all been going down well. Bored by now with my endless round of homemade soups, he made his own gazpacho yesterday, even going out himself to Beaminster to get the ingredients.

On top of that, he fancied chicken and chips, so made it all himself and thoroughly enjoyed the feast. Without after-effects! How brilliant is that. And today he was still upbeat and comfortable. Yay!

Then he started saying, 'When I am better...' which filled me with fear. I knew he knew what was going on and wasn't sure if he simply meant when he felt better than he does now, or if he actually thought there was a miracle heading our way on the horizon. I'm usually the optimistic, positive one whose glass is always half full, so this was hard for me. Of course I was ever hopeful we'd wake up one morning from this trauma and everything would go back to being gloriously, boringly normal. I wish...

But it may not. I knew that. It terrified me and so I felt hugely grateful for the times when he felt well, like now, because I didn't have to deal with all that yet. Not today anyway. And, as we were literally living day to day, that made life a lot easier. It's when he was feeling ill that the truth so viciously flooded in and it was so hard to clamber out of the mire.

So the sun was shining. His friend John popped in for a cup of tea and a chat. The front door was being replaced by some lovely local fitters and all was normal and well. You can't ask for more than that. Not today anyway...

26 May 2015

Hey, a great couple of days. Robin was feeling so much better he was almost eating normally – chicken and chips (gorgeous homemade yummies with crispy outside and meltingly soft inners, eat your hearts out, superchefs!). There seemed to be no discomfort on swallowing or getting the food down which all augured well for the tumour shrinking, we hoped. He was still eating reduced amounts but at least he was getting good food down so that was brilliant in the goodness stakes.

Then from all that to two days of down and out. It was the hospital wot dunnit. We went to Dorchester to see the consultant, as you do prior to your next chemo bashing. It should have been straightforward and brief. Brief yes, straightforward no. I'd kept a note of Robin's reactions and side effects following the first onslaught of chemo drugs. The consultant was kind but didn't seem especially interested in my endeavours. He listened to Robin's recall of the vomiting, nausea, weakness, shaking etc, etc and then said they'd alter the nausea meds prior to his next session and keep this going, all being well, for the six cycles and then perhaps give him a break. And did he want to ask him any questions. He asked that twice.

I asked if the trembling and shaking was normal. He said it might have been a small infection and was he okay now? Yes. Okay then.

No other questions popped into our minds. Apart from the obvious elephant in the room, of course.

So that was it. The consultant said he was on holiday next week so would see Robin in four weeks and good luck in the meantime.

Okay. We had planned to look at a sculpture garden after the hospital. It was gorgeous. Stunning sculptures skilfully choreographed round beautiful lakes, full spring weather – what could be nicer...

Everything. Robin felt ill and rubbish. I think it was the thought of the 'six cycles' and the word 'break'. It meant there was a lot more to come, 'all being well' of course. He told me he didn't want to live and die on chemotherapy. I was happy to die then and there. The heavy stone in my belly came back. Reality was kicking in big time again.

He was ill the next two days till the raging monster relaxed inside him. He started to feel hungry and wanted to cook. Our old pal Mark came to stay, the first friend in several months, and Robin was brilliant. Bright, funny, healthy, hungry – you'd never have thought there was a thing wrong with him. Just occasional fatigue, when he had a rest, but otherwise great.

By now it seemed we were learning *to live WITH cancer* instead of *dying FROM cancer*. It's always been my passion to play with words and now this simple tweak in emphasis changed the very nature of the burden we were carrying.

I realised I couldn't go on carrying the adrenalin-filled terror that fear of the future inflicts. I knew that 'living for the moment' was the best way to be and, as a complementary therapist, it's the way of being I'd strived for over many years. I understood the concept, but I'd never completely achieved it.

Now the simplicity of that phrase slapped me in the face. There *was* no other way to be. I saw the fear and shock in other people's faces and I'm sure they wondered how we were being so calm. The heavy stone in the pit of my stomach still lurched about in the early hours and I often felt the prickle of impending tears as I crossed a distant field with the dog. But I couldn't live like that all the time. I had to get on and be there for Robin. I couldn't pretend it didn't all exist or that it'd go away in a day or two. But we were learning pretty fast that this was now far more about living than dying. I just wished it hadn't taken me this long and this way to learn it.

16 June 2015

I haven't written for a few weeks because, well just because…

The second chemo cycle was more up and down than the first. Robin emerged from the hospital barely able to walk or speak, and felt both numb and painful. Grateful for small blessings, there was at that stage no nausea. They'd given him a strong anti-emetic even before the chemo drips were attached and that worked for a couple of days. Then just as his voice and limbs started behaving normally, the nausea kicked in with a vengeance. He wasn't able to eat for days while the district nurses vainly tried various meds to help him.

Nothing seemed to touch it, and though the nurses were great, the onslaught of so much medication over that first week became untenable and R's immune system took a nosedive. With a low white cell count and an infection setting in, he just wanted to sleep 24/7 and was urgently admitted to hospital where they tried to sort him out for four long days.

It was a stressful, dark time for those of us looking on. The daily 45-minute drive to and from the hospital was lightened only by the insanely gorgeous countryside I whizzed through. The dog was beside herself waiting for her beloved master to come home, rushing past me to the car every time I got back only to slink back into the house, head bowed, when she realised he wasn't there.

At least Robin was in the right place, with people who knew what they were doing and who were trying their best to help him. We hoped. After several traumatic nights for him, he suddenly started feeling better and, joy of joys, was discharged on Friday evening.

Freya literally cried with delight when she saw him get out of the car. She couldn't, wouldn't leave him alone and showed him beyond all doubt how much she loved and adored him. She wasn't the only one...

The next few days were much better as he became stronger and was eating better – normally at first and then voraciously. The weight that had dropped off him started coming back and life took on a 'normal', even happy, dimension.

Everyone asked how he was and seemed amazed by my cheerful, upbeat manner. I'd learnt that living for the moment literally means being happy when you have something to be happy about. I knew there were things to worry about and fear, but that was for later and this was for now. I love him, he was better than he'd been for months and we were both happy bunnies. We even went out and bought a new car we've been looking at for some time. So there.

Later that day...

We've just been to see the oncologist and, well, here's what he said...

'Let's stop the chemotherapy for now.' I nearly fell off my chair though, thankfully, this time didn't faint. Were they abandoning him? Thinking there's no hope? Go home and die?

No, no, no. That wasn't it. After my initial panic and confusion, brain back in gear, I asked why.

The consultant explained that as Robin was feeling well and eating properly, it seemed the first two cycles of chemo had done a significant amount of work. He wanted to build on that, get Robin's strength back, give him a chemo-free summer with regular blood tests, scans and checks, until the tumours kicked in again. Then they'd consider more chemo, but this time tailor it more effectively so (hopefully) it wouldn't make him feel so ill.

Looking at my confused face, he also explained that it's usually the first two cycles of chemo drugs that do the most work, and that thereafter, it's mostly picking away at the edges. Like cutting an apple in half, he said. You get rid of most of the apple with the first and second cut, then it's just increasingly smaller pieces after that.

Oh. Okay. I think.

The consultant also said that Robin was 'exquisitely sensitive' to the drugs and that it seemed the tumours were, too, so that they'd responded very quickly to the treatment so far.

Robin was over the moon about not having to go through chemo again two days later as previously planned. I needed to think about it a bit more.

Interestingly and reassuringly, everyone was delighted when we told them – even the former cancer sufferers and medics among our friends and family. I started to think it must be okay then. We were both very positive and started to live life NOW and EACH DAY, and fantastically we were both extraordinarily happy and 'healthy'.

I realised over those next few weeks how good life can be when those you love are happy. Glasses half full all over the house – no half empties anywhere in sight. I even began to wonder if Robin had forgotten he had cancer and thought perhaps he'd live for ever. It worried me that he might have a helluva shock when told by some well-meaning doctor or nurse that it was all still there, lurking.

9 July 2015

Robin had his next CT scan down in Dorchester just to check how it's all going. Even I, who's usually desperate to know everything about everything, was now not quite sure I wanted the results. Robin was a little quiet for the first time in several weeks, probably grappling with memories of previous hospital visits and stays. We cheered ourselves up by walking down by the river in Dorchester (a hidden treasure) and then enjoying a Japanese lunch in a new little place just opened in the centre. Robin said his sushi was to die for. Let's hope not.

12 July 2015

For the first time in many months, even before the C word came into our lives, Robin experienced pain in his upper abdomen. He was naturally worried and emotional thinking it was coming back, but it was way too soon. His back was also bad, an old injury from years ago, and he put two and two together thinking the big C may have spread into his spine. I tried to be positive and reassuring. It could just be bad indigestion and his bog standard backache. We looked at each other, worried, walked the dog, watched the men's final at Wimbledon, anything and everything to take our minds off the grim possibilities.

Next day all was well. Friends came round for lunch. Robin

was fine, the dark cloud had passed over and the sun was shining. We had a week before seeing the consultant and were determined to enjoy it. Yes, yes, yes...

It's interesting that I used to find uncertainty very hard to deal with. I'd rather know all the facts so I could attempt to be in control. It was always the 'unknowingness' of situations that floored me. I always thought that if I knew what was going on I could deal with it. Now I realised that learning to be comfortable with 'not knowing' is one of my life's greatest challenges. Letting go the need to know was excruciatingly hard but maybe I was getting there. I now knew that living right here right now took precedence over wasting time worrying what was going to happen tomorrow. Hmm.

I was also learning to respond rather than react when I heard about things outside my control. It's all about trusting and going with the flow. It's a pretty turbulent journey, I knew, but somewhere I felt the flow would take us all home. Just please not quite yet...

4 August 2015

After having a nice time basking in the glow of not knowing the results of the scan yet, seeing friends, going out places and generally living 'normally' for a change, 21 July came and we headed off down to Dorchester to see the consultant. Robin had been feeling so well, better than he'd been all year, that it was hard to contemplate the cancer having got worse or having spread. But the scan would tell all. Neither of us slept much the night before.

It was strangely quiet in the car, as with so many of our journeys to the hospital. When we went in, the consultant was smiling and it just got better from there. The scan showed the tumours had reduced in size and that the chemo had done a good job. The consultant was pleased with Robin's progress and said it was *our* job to go and live our lives and *his* job to monitor the situation. So he made an appointment to see Robin again in two months with another scan scheduled for two months after that.

I could barely believe my ears as he was talking about September and November, months I'd hardly dare dream about several months ago. He even said that in a couple of months he expected Robin would just walk in and say he was feeling fine and that the scan in four months was just to check all was well. Any further chemo could be arranged as and when needed in the future (wow, the 'future' word!) but would this time be tailored better, based on his last experiences so as not to be so crippling.

He did say, of course, that it all depended on how Robin was feeling and to get in touch in the meantime if anything worried him. He told Robin not to worry about little twinges. But if things go on for longer or get worse, just let him know and he would always make time to see him.

We floated out to the car and just sat there. Relief and joy washed over us. It wasn't the end of the journey, nothing like, but at least for the time being all was well, better than well, and happy times were a real possibility.

And so it was over the next few weeks. We had friends and family to stay, we went to the coast and across the fields, scoured the local National Trust gardens and countryside walks, and ate anything and everything to our hearts' content. Who knew life could be so full of simple pleasures.

The garden was looking glorious after all Robin's hard work and everything was flourishing and flowering as if to celebrate the lives being lived in this house.

Robin wanted to organise a holiday but we had two problems. First is that I didn't know whether I'd be okay to fly until after I saw the haematology consultant on 11 August about my pulmonary embolisms earlier in the year. I was feeling perfectly fine now, but they needed to establish whether my blood has any weird tendencies to clot or not. And second, we had to find some way of getting travel insurance without taking out a mortgage because of Robin's cancer and my heart.

Great eh? Just when we were both well enough to go celebrate in the sun, it looked like we'd have to pay through the nose for the privilege. However, we were doing our research on this and were sure there'd be a way.

15 October 2015

Okay, so we didn't get to go abroad to the sun but it wasn't because of insurance or flights. We just fancied staying nearer to home in glorious Dorset and who could blame us. The summer was great, not as hot or with long languid days like last year, but lush and relaxing none the less.

Robin loved being outside and did loads in the garden, Freya had some wonderful walks over fields and hills, on beaches and along brooks. Robin was eating well and we were going out with friends, having people to stay and loving our village life.

We lived from day to day, making no plans, just going with the flow.

But then the symptoms started returning. Intermittently at first and then with more persistence. Robin was getting the familiar discomfort when eating, feeling tired and listless and eventually complained of the foul taste in his mouth he'd had before. We were due to see the consultant on 22 September, and after another CT scan, he confirmed what Robin already knew, that the cancer was back.

It was a huge kick in the stomach, but not unexpected. The chemo regime they suggested this time was to be more gentle, bearable and continuous. Instead of the big blast of drugs at the hospital once every three weeks, Robin was fitted with a picc line in his arm that would slowly deliver the drugs continuously through a pump. It was the size of a baby's bottle and became known as Pablo the Pump.

Robin and Pablo soon became *The Odd Couple* and got to

know each other well. Showers and sleeping were interesting, but Robin managed it all well. He spent the first couple of days in bed feeling nauseous and knocked out, but after day three he got up and walked the dog. Eating was still a problem but we were going for little and often, soft and smooth. Our friends and neighbours were brilliant, turning up at the door with soups and sorbets, ice cream and fruit fools.

We went once a week for refits, when Pablo was changed for a newer, younger model. At first we could do that here in Bridport rather than going over to Dorchester – a great bonus when the refit itself only took minutes. We got to know the chemo nurses well and I, especially, found it very reassuring being able to talk with them about Robin's progress and reactions. Karen and Abby were more lovely and helpful than they could possibly know.

And then...

It was round about this point that I lost the will to sit here writing about what was happening and instead became wholly wrapped up in just living it. Looking back now, it seems all a bit of a blur. I can recall the highest highs and the lowest lows, not because of what was written in the diary but because of how they felt and the impact they had on us.

After some months of being with his new friend Pablo the Pump, Robin began suffering more and more from nausea and was less and less interested in eating. He had a scan which showed that the drugs were working well in slowing the disease down and the consultant suggested a break from the treatment for a while. He suggested Robin visit the specialist palliative doctors at the local hospice to see if they could help get the nausea under control.

The Joseph Weld Hospice, like many others, radiates kindness and care the moment you walk through the door – it feels positive and safe, and we felt welcome and comfortable in a way that a big busy hospital could never match. Robin's stay there made him feel calmer and more relaxed, especially since the food he ate was both fantastic and edible. Their suggestions for treatments were full of possibilities, I was able to visit any time, and as dogs were also welcome I could take Freya too. She was an instant hit with the staff, and it was heart-melting to see her squeal and wiggle with pure joy to see her dad.

Dr Helen and Dr Paul managed the impossible and Robin felt well enough to come home after a few days. We then heard that unfortunately for us, our hospital consultant was leaving for pastures new in Australia and we instead saw an enthusiastic locum oncologist. She was upbeat and eager to get Robin on some new trials at The Royal Marsden in London, or possibly Southampton. She said they would let us know directly and to stay off the chemo until we heard.

Over the next few weeks we waited and waited, then waited some more. We heard nothing from the Marsden or Southampton, though the oncologist phoned Robin at home several times to see how he was. Not good.

Shortly after that, a new consultant oncologist came on board at DCH. She was down-to-earth and positive and talked about the possibility of trying a promising new immunotherapy treatment if Robin had the 'right kind' of tumour cells. So, another endoscopy and biopsy followed. The results were good – he was HER2 positive, and after an echocardiogram to check his heart was okay, they started the treatment with Herceptin immunotherapy and chemotherapy.

It went surprisingly well, didn't knock him out and after the first treatment we even stopped for lunch at our favourite cafe Aroma in Bridport – we hadn't been able to do that for months. Things were looking promising.

As it turned out, it seems it was all *too* good. The Herceptin and chemo worked so well that the secondaries in the liver were actually being killed off. Great cause for celebration, you'd think.

But no, the mass areas of dead cells were becoming a hotbed for potential infection and poor Robin was in and out of hospital with spiking temperatures and on intravenous antibiotics for days and sometimes weeks. He became weaker and more bedbound.

They took him off the treatment, hopefully temporarily, and he had another CT scan to check what was going on.

3 November 2016

It's hitting me now. After the good news a couple of months ago that the tumours were dying as a result of the immunotherapy and chemo, the tough news now was that the latest CT scan showed the liver secondaries were growing again.

It was hard to take. Especially as it was quickly followed by Robin saying calmly and clearly that he'd done with chemo and didn't want any more drug intervention. He was weak from all the marauding toxins in his system and just wanted out.

It was hard for me to hear, but I understood and couldn't blame him. I was amazed that after he had made that decision he seemed completely at peace. He said it was a relief to make the decision and to know where he was at, and would now just concentrate on quality of life for whatever time he had left.

Of course, none of this was unexpected or surprising given what we'd been through over the last year and a half. And yet, for me, it was still a huge shock and felt like I'd been kicked in the belly. I've been online checking out all the new treatment and drug options (there weren't any really) but I had to accept that Robin was adamant he wanted nothing else. It's his choice. And I respected that, even though there was a silent storm raging inside me.

The tough bit was telling everyone. And accepting the inevitable shock and sadness that created. The family knew right away and were stoic and supportive, but it was hard for them too. I tried to keep all that at arm's length because we had enough stuff of our own to deal with right now. I wanted Robin to have as good and easy a time as possible over this last period. He was so loved by all, the premature outpourings were inevitable. But I was clear that we had to make this as easy as we could for him and deal with our own issues and upsets later. That was vital and my highest priority, however hard it got. I loved, adored and admired him – and I just hoped I was up to the task...

25 November 2016

It's hard to watch someone you love and know so well becoming distant and occasionally grumpy. He said he didn't feel connected to any of us anymore. He once described it like being alone in a white box. All he wanted was to find the right door so he could get out.

It was hard for everyone. People wanted to rush round here and, when they did, were full of sadness and emotion. They cried and said how strong I was being – but of course I wasn't.

His sister Lynne was the only one who had an inkling what it was like living with this day by day. She came down regularly from Banbury to see her beloved brother and help out. We had become united and I was so grateful for her visits. She and Robin had always been close, so each time she came was a beautiful balm for us all.

Later on...

Once again, I couldn't continue writing the running commentary as we were too busy just being in it. It seemed we were at that place they used to mark on old maps: 'Beyond here there be dragons'. There were dragons – and much more.

In retrospect, it was life-changing peaks and troughs, like a scramble across the Himalayas. Robin was brilliant and brave. I was knackered and frustrated. Fortunately we had lovely community nurses who came in regularly. The hospice doctors and nurses were always available if we needed them and offered to take him into the hospice any time if he wanted to go back there.

Robin chose to stay at home. There were, occasionally, beautiful unexpected moments. I loved him so much but could do so little to make all this better. I felt if I kept telling him how much he was loved it would somehow give him strength and nurture that vital energy he needed to deal with the shit life was now throwing at him. It didn't.

He became increasingly weak and in pain, and I became increasingly frustrated and angry at the disease that was taking him away from me. The doctors, nurses and carers who came round were a real lifeline, experienced and understanding of our daily challenges and pulling out all the stops to get Robin what he needed so he could stay here at home. They were brilliant with both of us and my frustrations soon melted into just helping and supporting my lovely husband. Lynne was now coming to stay every week, helping more than she'll ever know just by being here and loving us both.

Christmas came and went. New year drifted by barely noticed.

And so here we are now. All those months ago back in April 2014, the gastroenterology consultant suggested Robin had only months to live. But our unique, special and much-loved man managed to stay here with us for another 21 months before finally going home on 9 January 2017. He slipped away for his next adventure in the arms of his sister and me, in his own bed and with his ever-loving dog Freya by his side.

Celebrations and Sadness

I'm not going to write much about the funeral (awful, surreal word) except to say that so many people came it ended up being quite a squeeze and a celebration. I was amazed how many people had travelled far and wide to be there, and Robin himself would have been moved and delighted by the outpourings of love for him – I'm sure he had no idea he'd touched so many lives and made such deep impressions.

With music being so much part of him all through his life, he chose his own tracks for this final goodbye – *Sometimes It Snows in April* by Prince, *Little Wing* by Jimi Hendrix and *Can't Make a Sound* by Elliott Smith. Then there was room at the end for one more piece – what, out of so many? His good friend Brett suggested Santana's *Oye Como Va*, a bouncy number which he said would have them dancing in the aisles as they left the chapel...

It was a humanist celebration and the tributes were given by those who loved him – his sister Lynne and nieces Becky and Cheryl, his schoolfriend and old mate Pete and also, if I could get through it, me. Robin also wanted to write his own message to everyone, so here's what was on the back of everyone's Order of Service:

A message from Robin...

And so you may have gathered that I am only here in spirit with you today, having written this before I start my journey to the next place. Although this list of people and memories may not be totally comprehensive and I apologise if I've left anyone out, it is the best I can do after a long, magical and speedy life in the fast lane.

My love and thanks go out to all the following people: my beautiful wife Helly, my sister Lynne and her fantastically practical husband Phil (thank you for all your help over the years), the amazing Rebecca and CK and their partners, my 'brother-from-another-mother' Mark with whom all my conversations have been both warm and illuminating, also Anne and Steve, Jan and Colin and all their brilliant boys and girls (thank you so much for all your support and for making me feel so welcome into the family). Special mention also to Yvie and Paul and to all my ex-Cuckfield friends and neighbours, a big thank you for all the love, and to our witnesses at our wedding Andy and Jane and all those wonderful Thai meals we shared, every one of them fabulous, even in that grotty pub. Also to Trisha and Margaret, Corinne, Carol, Anna and all our lovely south-east buddies and the gang from Oriel school.

To all my personal friends who always gave me love without condition, I salute you: Bec, Simon, Brett, Anthony, Peter, Linda, Pete, Sue – the finest friends a man could have. I look back to those heady days of the 70s and 80s when I was managing Rock Dreams and would like to thank with a happy heart all my staff, customers and anyone who ever ventured near our shops for giving me an overpaid hobby that filled my life with such joy and also allowed me to go to 100s of the greatest gigs ever seen in London (and yes I was there at the Rainbow on that Sunday afternoon when Little Feat blew the Doobie Bros off the stage and also saw Jimi Hendrix do the same to the Who at the Saville Theatre in Shaftesbury Avenue).

And finally we moved here to Drimpton in July 2014 and stepped right into the heart of a proper community that accepted us wholeheartedly and without question. Our wonderful dog Freya immediately became part of the walking elite of the village and we were soon partaking of all the foodie delights around which our village's social life is seemingly built (Rosemary thank you for the bacon butties and everyone for all the delicious bakes...).

Since becoming ill, I can genuinely say I have been overwhelmed by the support and caring from practically everyone in the village and it has really helped me get through some of the darker days. So a big thank you to all the following: John, Pat, Martin, Julie, Mel, Maurice, Diana, Alyson, Jenny, Eddie, Molly, Deirdre,

Derek, Denis, Rosanna, Gina, George, Viv, John, Christabel, Terry for the best eggs, Norman, Jane, Neville, Anna, Ann, Jim, Alan, Janice, Peter, Joyce, Roger, Linda, David, Rae, Mary, Dermott and everyone. Thank you people, you really helped.

And now I think you should go and have a drink and sandwich and celebrate because I'm in a happier place now. Thank you...

My own tribute came at the end. I did manage to get through it (just...) with a solid hand squeeze and support from our dear friend Kathryn who'd led our wedding blessing all those years ago...

Helly's tribute to Robin...

Robin was a man of many parts. And, since he left us, it's been a real light in the darkness for me to see how so many other people saw him and felt about him. What a guy. It's lovely to share our own experiences of knowing and being with him – we each have our personal memories and treasured moments.

He would often skim stones across the water and I can see now that the ripples he created through his life have spread far and wide, touching us all in their own special way.

Robin was my husband and, more lately, my hero – though I never imagined he'd be either when we first met in a pub all those years ago in Ardingly. He had that initially shy winning smile and impish twinkle in his eye. He was edgy and unique, generous and kind. All the best combinations. And I wasn't the only one who thought so, obviously, as so many of you are here.

After his somewhat wild life in the fast lane, it's strange to think of this warm-hearted renegade choosing to tuck himself tightly into a tiny cottage in the country with a busy new wife, five cats and a dog. But he took to it right away. We both did. His relaxed and instinctive understanding of people meant he made friends with ease and my friends and family all loved him. He could talk with anyone about anything, especially if it involved music, gardening, food, wine, teddy bears, watches, steam trains or classic old liners. Sparky, bright and witty, he was also one of the kindest and most generous people I've ever met.

His collection of artist's and designer bears also moved into our small space, along with cases of antique watches and endless CDs, and somehow it all just worked. Like it was meant to be.

He quickly started creating a magical space out of my wild garden, just as he's been doing here in Dorset. He threw himself into things and did everything with great love and enthusiasm. I loved so much about him. His cooking became legendary and, although a meat eater himself, took to creating delicious vegetarian dishes and discovering new wines with enthusiasm.

I'm sure he's gob-smacked and delighted at how many of us are here today. He wanted a simple send off – he chose the funeral directors and the music, and was totally ready and waiting to join his late great musical heroes for what we called the great gig in the sky. Then he wrote his personal message to you all on the back of your order of service.

He asked me to tell you:

'When I was ill here at home, I was thinking that now I'm finally able to go to the great gig in the sky and watch the greatest band ever of Prince, David Bowie, Lemmy and John Bonham – and that makes me very happy. As Jimi said, "See you in the next one. Don't be late..."'

My Robin and yours was special in every way – a deeply loved person who spread so much joy and happiness. He said to me once, completely out of the blue, that our greatest role in life was to love and be loved. He achieved that in spades.

I love some of the wise comments that have come in his many cards and messages.

'Grief is love with no place to go, but it is our proof that we loved.'

'It is hard to imagine a world without our beautiful Robin, but then I smile at the thoughts and memories that flood my mind and *realise, of course, he will always be here.'*

'It's hard to forget someone who gave you so much to remember.'

'It will be tough for you right now and for a while ahead, but I sense that what you gained from having Robin in your life was, and is, the greatest treasure of all.'

'Deep in our hearts your memory is kept, we loved you too deeply to ever forget.'

So thank you, Robin, for all you are and all you were and all you gave us. And thank you everyone who held both of us in your hearts throughout this last challenging journey. Enjoy the gigs, Robin. My love goes with you…

Where Do We Go From Here...

Robin's 'celebration' was a great success – apparently. It helped me, I think, to have something to work on – a great responsibility to get it right and do this last earthly thing for him. After that, it all became a bit of a blur.

Amid the blur, though, was the realisation I had to get the 'business bits' properly organised and everything transferred into my name. Robin had done all he could to 'put his affairs in order', and even made notes for me to make this as straightforward as possible. But neither he nor I had figured that, although everything was so clear-cut and simple, I would have to get probate in order to reorganise his and my accounts.

'Blur begone, I have work to do,' I felt like screaming. So the next couple of months were punctuated by not much sleep, the inevitable ups and downs (well, mostly downs) of grieving, as well as endless toings and froings with service providers, banks and building societies. Fortunately I had sympathetic folk around who helped and encouraged, and finally I got where I was going. Sorted, but not somewhere I wanted to be. Sadly.

There's so much online and in self-help books about the best way to deal with loss. I read a lot (what else could you do at 2.30am?) and there was loads of advice about the stages you go through, the time scales, coping strategies etc. I stopped after a while as much of it made me feel worse. We're all so different. Nothing works for everyone. I realised early on I'd have to do it my way.

I found it especially tough coping with the up-and-down, never-know-where-you-are nature of grief. And the big black hole you suddenly fall into just when you thought you were doing okay.

But I was still here (a phrase Robin used most mornings when he woke up). I hadn't killed myself yet, but then I didn't have the time or the energy. I was continually knackered because there was such a lot of other stuff to do. Not just surviving the storm raging inside me, but so much organising and sorting. I was doing things, endlessly doing things. I imagined everyone was expecting me to fall apart, so I didn't. Not then anyway.

Some days when I seemed to be doing okay, out of the blue came the monsoon. The waterworks. The tsunami. Serious floods in the South West. It was the torrent that keeps on giving – I called it TES (tsunami eye syndrome). The tears whooshed, unbidden, unexpected. The slightest thing, not even anything to do with lovely Robin, and I'd be awash. Wherever I happened to be and whoever I happened to be with. Even when I was on my own – that's easier, of course, because I could just let it flow. But when I'm out? Not so easy.

So why did it just seem to be getting worse?

It felt like a reality check. Whatever I'd been doing to survive day by day since 'the event' had now slipped deeper into the torrid realisation that this is for ever. No respite or time off for good behaviour. No waking up from a bad dream. This is it, this is all there is. Life without him. Always and for ever.

It was a deep down heavy weeping. It was exhausting. It was all-pervading. It was depressing. But...

I had friends coming to stay on and off so I had to get up and get on. I needed to 'immaculate' the house. Make the beds. Get some food on. I hoped I could...

Well, I suppose I did because I'm still here (again). When Robin used to say that every morning it was a kind of joke at first, but towards the end he really wished he wasn't. He just wanted to go. Peacefully at night would have suited him fine. He'd had enough and could barely take any more. It hurt me to hear it but I loved him and I understood perfectly.

I understand better now how much our parameters change when we're faced with traumatic situations. It's why, I think, I could never truly judge those who we consider make 'strange' or 'questionable' decisions in difficult situations we have no experience of. Who are we to judge when we have no idea what they were going through or how they felt. It's fine to have opinions, however honest and ethical, when we're sitting comfortably in our lounges with our families around us. Not necessarily the best recipe for being critical.

So here I am, up and down again. If I wasn't so busy getting on with things, I'd have been thoroughly seasick on this rollercoaster. But tomorrow is another day. Tomorrow may be better. I'll travel hopefully.

Time for the wishbone tree...

Notes

*1. *As I reread this diary, I can see that the joy I felt was about the possibility of having him with me for longer. The chemo regime was a way we could keep the cancer at bay, something we had no idea about following the gastroenterology consultant's gut-wrenching news. Now, with the benefit of hindsight, I can see for Robin it may have looked more like an appalling future feeling crap on heavy drugs leading only to the inevitable conclusion. But that's not quite how it went...*

*2. *The herbs were a mix of burdock root, slippery elm bark, sheep sorrel herb and turkey rhubarb root, often known as Essiac, which can help to support the immune system and have been reported to reduce the growth of tumours. The dried herbs are brewed together and bottled so they can be taken as a daily tonic.*

Tales From the Wishbone Tree

Part Two

Tales From the Wishbone Tree

The wishbone tree is a simple but special place in the wilds of West Dorset. It's set on high ground with to-die-for views (he did), and we scattered Robin's ashes there ('ashes' still sounds so surreal...) I go there a lot to sit and stare, to think, to wish for better things, to talk to Robin and to listen. Thoughts, feelings, plans and messages trickle (and sometimes rush) through my mind. These are just a few of them...

No plans...

Walking with Freya on the hill is about all I can do some days. It helps me think. Focus. The quiet and solitude is undemanding and comforting. I realise now that living a day at a time means I've lost the ability to think beyond tomorrow. It's anathema to me to make plans, write appointments in a diary, commit myself to anything in the future, tomorrow or next week, never mind next month or beyond. It's now all about being spontaneous, but only when the time is right. It's about going out and then, suddenly, wanting to run home. It's 11 weeks today since he left, and yesterday was worse than ever. The clocks going forward for spring is usually a time of celebration in our house – more daylight, longer evenings full of rambles and possibilities, spring ready to burst and tantalising summer on its way – positive, bright and happy.

But not this time. I had the ability in winter to hunker down, stay in, close the doors and shut the world out, hibernate, be alone with myself. These sunny days, though unquestionably gorgeous, just seem to open the wounds wider. Sunshine and evening light bring back memories of spur of the moment visits to the coast, exploring new places, new pubs and eateries, delicious drives, seeing friends, just heading out when we felt like it. Now that same brightness is making the looming 'emptiness' of long sunny days seem endlessly stark and bleak. Nowhere to hide.

So now raw hurt and pain puncture my nights. Then, as the tiredness leaves me more vulnerable, I just want to close the door to that ghoulish gaping future without him. I want to scream. My eyes are endlessly leaking and I now have just the slightest inkling why people choose to end it all, why 'going home' may seem infinitely preferable to staying here alone with the heartbreak.

I'm sure I wouldn't. I'm sure I couldn't. I know it'll pass. Soon...

There are messages on the phone I should reply to. But what can I say. Everyone I know, even those I love, seem so far removed from where I am now. I'm on a different planet and even though everyone's super sympathetic and lovely in their ways, all trying to help and make suggestions, no one can 'walk this path' but me. I know, understand and accept that I have to get through this myself.

So please, just for now folks, leave me alone. I'll try to do 'normal' when I've figured out some kind of future and can walk back in through the right door. I just can't deal with you as well as me right now. I'm full of grieving and that's just the way it is. For now.

Love cures all (I hoped)...

When you first discover your life partner isn't going to be with you for life after all, that your time together will soon be cut tragically short and your whole future snatched away, no words can reflect the thunderous storm that engulfs you.

One of my reactions was to tell Robin how much I loved him, all the time, over and over, as if knowing how much he was loved would somehow save him.

It helps me now to know he knew he was loved – not just by me but by so many others around him. I'm sure it helped. But save him? No. Sadly not.

So, later, when I sat alone by the wishbone tree, I was still talking to him:

'Do you remember how I told you I loved you all the time? I hoped maybe telling you how much you were loved would give you the energy and strength to carry on. As though the more love you had, the more comfortable and less ill you'd feel. So now here I am sitting on the grass at the wishbone tree looking out over your valley and it's just so beautiful. It's the perfect place to have scattered your ashes and given you back to the land you loved.

'There's the sea view you always wanted, over there is Charmouth and Golden Cap, someone's doing a bonfire; you have Colmers Hill, Chesil Beach and Portland in the distance, all very clear. The pond or lake we always wondered about is still an enigma, and there's Lewesdon Hill, Pilsdon Pen, and the school with the little windmill we always drove past. There's a huge blue sky, puffed up white clouds, buzzards and seagulls flying by and your faithful loving Freya lying here next to me as though there's no better place to be in the world.

'I love that she feels so comfortable up here and seems completely at home sitting by the wishbone tree as though she knows you're here. She instantly relaxes and stares into the distance. I miss you so much, though I know it's only early days. It's all very up and down, but at least I know you're not suffering anymore, and Freya and I will learn to live with the sorrow, I think. I know we'll be all right. We'll be all right as long as we're all right, and then sometime along the way we'll come and join you. That'll be good.

'The sun's twinkling on the sea down there at Charmouth, and the clouds are leaving shadows on the fields as they drift over. It's ever changing. And incredibly beautiful. You have such a beautiful spot here. It's stunning. Looking towards the sun like this reminds me of that Maori saying I heard recently: If you face towards the sun, your shadows are behind you. I like that.'

Robin's birthday

Everyone told me days like these would be the worst. Memories of better times. Birthdays and celebrations bringing up the past. Laying low, getting through another milestone without him.

Not for me, it seems. As every day without him is equally awful, the fact it's his birthday has made no difference. In fact, as it's turned out, the opposite is true.

I walked with Freya to the wishbone tree and sat there in the early morning light. The sun was already sparkling on the sea and the view over the valley was stunningly crisp and clear, way into the distance. It felt like a new day with fresh new insights. Yesterday's dark, dire thoughts were slowly dispersed by today's light. The deep pit of despair is less raw and today I feel full of gratitude. It's much less about what I've lost and much more about what I gained through knowing and being married to such a lovely man. Lucky me.

Robin slipped into my life simply and without fanfare, brought me joy and love without question, gave me strength and freedom to follow my heart, supported and secured me in love and comfort. He cherished and nurtured me and together we brought each other the crucial last pieces in our jigsaw of life.

We also brought each other peace and fun. Not to mention, of course, all the good food and wine, the laughs and adventures, the understanding and harmony, the joy of spending time together. Any occasional tiffs and frustrations always melted away as fast as they'd arisen, and we learned together what it's like to truly love and be loved. And I'm so grateful I had all that in my life.

One day the pain of losing him will be balanced by the joy of having had him. My memories of him will be a gift to treasure and not a burden to carry. I know it's true. I just have to sit with all this and work through it first. Every tear I shed for him is worth it. I wouldn't have missed the journey for the world.

There was a saying when I was young: 'No man is worth your

tears and the one who is, won't make you cry.' He didn't ever make me cry. It was the thing that took him away that made me cry.

The gift that goes on giving...

Sitting by the tree on that first birthday apart, I thought of the perfect gift for Robin and all those others who've moved on. I talked to him like he was just a step away...

'My eternal gift to you today and all days, darling, is love. Love and yet more love. You can never have too much, wherever you are. You gave me love in spades. I loved you then, now and always, that's a given.

'I was amazed by how you just "got me" from the start – you instantly understood me. And since you've moved on, many of your friends have said exactly the same. You had an instinctive understanding of people and effortlessly got on their wavelength. That's why we all loved you.

'I'm so grateful for everything we had. I thank you deeply from my whole heart. We were so lucky to have stumbled across each other when we did. We shared a great love for each other and for life, for nature and for animals, for art and music, for teddy bears and sports, and for our family and friends.

'So my gift to you today and always is love and gratitude, for all and everything...'

Another day, another angle...

I've begun to realise that this strange new life I'm living is more about being grateful for what we had rather than being destroyed by what I've lost. I'm thinking how amazing it was that we met at all. What a fluke. I know now that this excruciating loss is the price we pay for love. And I wouldn't have missed all those good times for the world. So if 'grief is the price we pay for love', Robin was worth it. Any price and every tear.

As there's nothing I can do about going through the terrible loss and emptiness, I'm going to have to somehow change the way I look at it. It's a bit like the 'glass half full, glass half empty' syndrome. I'm usually on the 'glass half full' side and that's all about the good stuff I had with Robin – joys and love, excitements and pleasures, companionship and warmth.

The glass half empty side is all about his absence – he's not here anymore and my life is bleak without him, no more hugs or adventures, just a looming empty future alone.

But sometimes my glass gets topsy-turvy and 'half full' becomes 'half empty' in the blink of an eye. I like the idea that whether the glass is half full or half empty, it obviously needs refilling. More wine. Yes, why not. I wish it were that simple.

I know now that absence is the greatest form of presence. He's with me every minute of every day, because I know he's not. One day I hope I can carry his memory as the special gift it is rather than this heavy grief-laden burden to bear. One day. Now, where's that wine…

Views from the other side…

I've been thinking about how we get through living with those we love when time is short but the hours are long. I would have done anything to ease Robin's journey (he hated that word and said it wasn't a 'journey' he wanted to be on). As his wife, carer, lover and friend, I was there with him every step of the way. But looking on *and* being part of it, I was both there in the middle *and* on the side. This was his journey, but mine too in so many ways.

The 'outside looking in' part is a tough place to be and I obviously wanted to do anything I could to alleviate his suffering. Being in it and living it day by day, it was hard to see any sort of big picture. We knew what the end would be but the luxury of making plans mostly eluded us. It was all about firefighting and dealing with each moment.

I wouldn't begin to describe to anyone how Robin was really feeling about it all, though I was there and saw the effects the disease and the treatments had on him, and we talked about it a lot. But I wouldn't put words into his mouth. I can only say it as I saw it.

Here by the wishbone tree, lots of things are becoming clear. We're all different. None of us is the same. Not in what happens to us, nor in our responses to it. Things for many people may look the same from the outside, but scratch the surface and we are all dealing with things individually and uniquely. So no two solutions to our situations can be the same. I'm especially aware of that now when I watch and hear people offering advice or making pronouncements based on their own experiences.

So if we're all on different journeys, we may see and feel the same things, but we all interpret them differently. We each have our own ways.

Any previous idea I might have had of how to deal with such a life-churning experience has definitely changed. One thing I feel strongly now is that when someone is dying, we should give them space to live – at whatever level that's possible. Instead of weighing them down and limiting them with our own ideas and 'stuff', I'd like to find a way of being that gives them peace, happiness, even moments of joy. Let their spirit fly.

So while someone's alive, I think they should have space to be themselves. Let them find their own way of dealing with things, make their own discoveries and find their own peace. Of course, support and love them, but not crowd or overwhelm or prescribe answers that may be right for us but maybe not for them. There's plenty of time later for us carers to cope with the fallout, the dark days and heartache.

I'm understanding this now, of course, because I've learned it sitting on the sidelines, watching the man I love going through it. I didn't get it all right – I wish I had. Would I do it differently now? Probably. But this is now my problem and I can bear it, even perhaps forgive myself for not being more patient and understanding.

One good thing is that the pain I feel now is only mine – I am no longer carrying Robin's suffering. He is free, released from pain and illness. That should make me feel better, I know. And sometimes it does, a little...

It's okay to be angry...

Another interesting development is that I've been tetchy and irritable with people recently and seem to be endlessly apologising for being bad-tempered. Walking the fields with Freya has thrown up another way of looking at this, and maybe I can begin to forgive myself for my bad moods...

Here's what came to me at the wishbone tree. Going through the grief thing is like being stripped bare, and I just can't do all the 'niceties' anymore. I only have resources for what I need to survive, so I suffer 'fools' (they're not, of course) less gladly than I probably did before.

I've been hoping that the irritability and the spikiness would go and I'd turn back into the warm, loving person I used to think I was. But I wonder whether that's just part of the learning process, that 'in extremis' all those fluffy niceties slip away and you become the naked essence of who you really are (though I'm hoping that doesn't mean I'm naturally bitter, angry and irritable...).

Perhaps it's just that my priorities are changing, or have already changed, so that I do what *feels right* rather than what is *expected*. And while I don't want to hurt anyone's feelings or upset anyone (I'd normally go a million miles to avoid that), I hope that after this I may be more honest and upfront about what I feel and what I want. Politeness is great, but honesty is better.

So maybe 'stripping bare' isn't necessarily a bad thing. I apologise to my nearest and dearest for being the grizzly grouch I've been recently, maybe not taking their care and consideration in the spirit it's intended. But perhaps that's just me becoming

47

more honest. Who knows. Maybe I'll find a balance, apologise where necessary but just be true to myself. I hope so...

Knitting a new life...

It's become blindingly obvious that life's emotional upheavals throw up all sorts of random discoveries/insights. It seems to me our lives are literally knitted together over time by our experiences and events. So each stitch, however small and insignificant it appears at the time, is vitally important. If we miss a step, perhaps we'll never get the whole picture.

It's always tempting to read a guide so we can quickly learn and fast-track through the grim bits, but I now feel that unless I go through the painful process properly I may never understand the lessons. The mind learns, but the heart remembers.

It also means that each one of us is vital in life's tapestry. If even a tiny stitch is lost, the picture may never be the same.

Walking with Freya through the village recently, I also realised how communities are literally knitted together, stitch by stitch, over time. When you move to a new place or a new job, it takes time to develop relationships with the people and the surroundings. We were particularly lucky moving here because various events caused it to happen naturally and quite quickly. But real community takes a while to develop deeply through shared experiences and days, weeks, months and years together.

You can't have a fabulous jumper without creating it stitch by stitch first. With people it's the same – it takes time to develop the 'stitches' in a community and they're stronger and more resilient because they've been knitted over time, often with compassion and love.

And now it's the same with my grieving – I have to do it a step at a time, sitting with the pain and going through it. It sometimes feels like it's destroying me but, in fact, I'm sure it's making me stronger, stitch by stitch, holding me together. I'm now learning not to avoid it or ignore it. Better to experience it, sit with it and go through it, knit more stitches to fill the holes and gaps, build me up and eventually create a stronger, more complete me. The sum of all my parts. The good and the not so good.

Let's hope that's worth waiting for...

Saved by bluebells...

After a challenging couple of days (it was that 'overwhelm' that just suddenly hits you and you can't crawl up out the black hole no matter what), I went for a walk with Freya to the wishbone tree.

As it was pretty early, there were only a few people about and we sat for a long time on the grass looking out at the stunning view. It was slightly hazy but the sun was already highlighting the edges of the clouds in the distance so they looked like shining, snow-capped mountains on the horizon.

I smiled because it looked magical even though I know there are no mountains there. And then the tears came again with the longing to share it with Robin. But I had to smile again because I knew he was there already.

After another while, Freya and I got up and went to another hill nearby which was covered in woods. As we walked through the trees, we were greeted by an amazing mass of bluebells bursting up in every direction. It was as unexpected as it was beautiful and I realised, as we were soon immersed in a profusion of flowers, I was suddenly feeling lighter and calmer. It was as if they just massaged the fear and anxiety away – my spirits lifted a little and I felt stronger and maybe more able to cope again.

Those bluebells saved me that day. Little things bring great joy when your world is collapsing. I hope I never stop noticing.

Riding the waves...

Walking with a neighbour and our dogs today, something dawned on me. It seemed like a significant discovery at the time.

If I was able make it through the grief thing by surviving one day at a time, perhaps I could use these 'survival' days better. If I knew I could survive the day ahead, maybe I could actually make use of the day in a more positive way. Perhaps doing a specifically good thing on those days would make me feel better?

Okay, hang on, I may not be ready to make 'future plans' for anything further than tomorrow, but if I felt up to it, I could decide each morning to do something that day that would bring some joy. It's such a little thing, but right now it seems like a good plan. We'll see...

Light and dark...

Another early morning surprise at the wishbone tree – walking across the hill in bright summer sunshine, suddenly the sky went dark and the clouds opened, drenching us few earlybirds with hard, heavy rain. I pushed on towards the brow of the hill and its usual stunning view, expecting it to be misty and wet, dark and gloomy. But instead, looking over the edge, it was like opening a door into another world. There at my feet, below the wishbone tree, the valley and the sea beyond stretched out in sparkling brilliance as if lit by some magic lamp. The contrast between darkness and light was sharp and staggering.

Far across the valley I could see the heavy clouds of rain drifting in, swallowing up the sunlight and creating darkness as they went. But behind them as they moved away, the bright light re-emerged and glistened even more intensely with reflections and shining flashes of water. It was magical.

A good photographer would have made a fortune here with studies of light and dark playing games across the countryside.

But for me it was just unexpectedly good to see this simple interplay between darkness and light. It seemed like a lesson for us all – something to remember when I feel 'in the dark' or gloomy. The sun is still there just out of sight and is likely to return even more brilliantly than before. It reminds me of another favourite old saying: 'Better to light a candle than curse the darkness.'

Then, just as I was marvelling at it all, the sun suddenly broke through the darkness on the hill where I was standing and shone down on Freya and me, illuminating the shiny wet ferns around the wishbone tree. I guess we need the darkness to appreciate the light.

Hindsight's a wonderful thing...

It's easy to say: 'If I'd known then what I know now, I would have done things differently.' How often have we all said that? With the benefit of hindsight and the wisdom of going through the experience, many of us know we could have reacted in better ways or chosen different paths and different ways of dealing with our traumas.

And yet it's *because* we had to deal with these things in the unknowingness and uncertainty of what was happening, we were the way we were. And, I guess, it's these very things that made us the people we are now.

There are so many 'how to' books out there – how to do this and how to get through that – written by people who undoubtedly know what they're talking about. But I reckon that unless you actually experience the things they're describing or go through the process yourself, you never truly get the wisdom. It takes time to digest and work through. I'm sure we'll get there eventually.

And here at the wishbone tree, Freya and I are sitting in bright sunshine but I can see dark clouds drifting across the valley. The weather here always seems to mirror what I'm feeling and the clouds look like they're bringing their curtains of rain this way. Time to move on...

Looking on the bright side...

On one of those bleak sort of days, I went up to the wishbone tree for some peace and solace. The sky is huge on the hill and you can see for miles across Dorset. I sat with Freya, staring idly into the distance. The weather was dull and for me life looked pretty grey.

Then I noticed a tiny chink of light in the distance and somewhere inside me I heard the words: 'Always check for the chink of light, however small it seems. Maybe it's a sign there's more light to come – or perhaps it's a crack in the door. One day when you're ready, that could be a door you could open...'

I immediately thought of something Leonard Cohen used to say – that there's a crack in everything, that's how the light gets in. I really hoped so...

It also reminded me how people say, 'When one door closes, another opens.' I used to smile about that, too, because many of us are usually looking in the wrong direction and never see it. So maybe if I just turned round occasionally, I might just see that chink of light through the crack. And then who knows?

So thank you, Leonard, and thank you, wishbone tree, here I go travelling hopefully again...

Life after death...

There is a life after death – for those of us left behind anyway. I'm beginning to see that now. It's not a life I've chosen and it's not one I particularly want, but I can feel it starting to stretch out before me. But it's a life without Robin, so who'd want to live there?

I suppose it's a bit like moving somewhere new – beginning again, things unfamiliar, hankering after the past and the nostalgia, trying to get used to the new place and different ways of doing things. After a while I imagine they'll become familiar and it won't seem so alien or strange.

Maybe there might even be parts of it I could like or begin to enjoy. It's tough to see that just now, but who knows. I'll never forget my old life, I'll never forget the joys I had living here with

Robin – and I'm nowhere near ready yet to move on. But I have begun to realise that life is continuous and there is something more along the road. And I guess I'll go through that door when I'm ready. Not yet, but maybe sometime.

One day perhaps I'll be able to relocate Robin in my life and take his precious memory with me wherever I go. He'll always be part of me and who I am, and I'll be able to smile every time I think of him. One day…

Life rolls on…

Sitting by the wishbone tree gives me time to think outside the box. Today (and perhaps more and more) I'm feeling the deepening connection between nature and my own life. I've always known we are 'part of' not 'apart from' nature and I can see that birth and death are the two bookends that support our experiences here on earth. They're both a vital part of our life's cycle and you can't have one without the other. It's blindingly obvious every time you look at nature – the changing seasons, the renewal and regrowth, birth and death in an endless circle.

So whether we're atheists and simply leave our bodies to the worms when our lives are over, or whether we believe our spirit or essence lives on when its physical journey here on earth is concluded, nature seems pretty clear that death engenders new life.

Personally, I like to think my body is the 'vehicle' I travel in through this earthly life, and that when I die, I'll simply park it up somewhere (a crematorium probably) and go back home where I came from. I love the old Hollywood movie *The Wizard of Oz* with Judy Garland singing her heart out in *Over the Rainbow*. That'll be me, over there with the bluebirds. Let's hope that's where Robin is, too.

Never alone…

Another day by the wishbone tree and today I was feeling

especially alone, although lovely Freya was there beside me as usual. I don't know what I'd do without her – she gets me up in the morning, she takes me for walks, she snuggles up on the sofa, what more could I need...

But then I felt that voice inside again – Robin telling me that whenever I go anywhere on my own, I should remember he's right there with me. I instantly smiled – what a great idea. Why hadn't I thought of it before? I could easily imagine him at my side as I tussle with the usual social situations.

I must try it. I'll muddle through. I'll just keep telling myself: 'Whenever I go somewhere on my own, I'll remember you're right there beside me. Every time I feel alone, I'll remember you're with me.'

I will. I wish...

Sharing love...

A quick thought while walking back over the hill – thanks to my years of being with Robin, I've had a glorious time full of personal love and hand-holding. So maybe, now that's all sadly changed, it's time to open up again, look outwards and share that love with the world. They say grief is love with nowhere to go. But the world is crying out for love. I must get to work redirecting it into useful, compassionate ways to help others. Hugs anyone?

Future forecast...

The sky over the wishbone tree always has something to say. Today the weather was overcast when I left home, but up here on the hill it feels like I'm actually walking in the cloud itself. It's densely misty and wet, though when I look down it's dry in the valley. It seems strange as I get to the wishbone tree that the whole distant view is covered with cloud, but immediately just below the hill at my feet everything is crystal clear.

More lessons here then. It seems that though we may be able

to see clearly up to the next step in our life (like today), beyond that is a mystery.

This is tricky for me. I've always found it unsettling not knowing about things – not for me the surprise party. What, everyone knew except *me*??? What a nightmare. Robin hated that I never wanted surprises – no thank you. I'm not good with it, I want to know what's going on.

So all the uncertainty and 'unknowingness' of Robin's illness was yet another reason why it was all so hard to deal with – on many levels and in so many ways. I'd want to know everything about everything, but I was soon forced to accept this isn't what life and death situations are all about. In the end I actually found myself *not* wanting to know the what and how and when. A complete change of heart for me. That's how much these experiences change us. On all levels and in all ways.

But here today is a simple vision of my view of the future. I can see just in front of me but I can't see way into the distance or any further forward. So that's it. Why worry about a future you can't see? They say if you can't change the situation you're in, try changing the way you look at it. So, instead of seeing my new future as solitary and fearful, perhaps I should look at it differently. I could think: 'Okay, I can't see what's going to happen, but maybe it'll be okay. Who knows.'

So perhaps the future is full of possibilities and not terrifying things. Perhaps we can just tweak the way we see things so they don't look so awful. And here we are back at that half empty/half full glass again – and, yes okay, it just needs refilling...

Keep it simple stupid (KISS)...

I was walking away from the wishbone tree when it came to me. Simple words, making sense.

This year, keep it simple. Sort stuff, be kind, give myself time to get to know the new me. No pressure, no hurry.

Go slow, go forward – welcome in this strange new single

person called 'me'.

Home at home...

Instead of spending all my time missing Robin, I'm trying to find a way to relocate him in my life. It's hard not seeing him crossing the kitchen or coming downstairs, or being out in the fields or down at the beach. He may not be physically here with me anymore, but he'll always be part of me, part of my life and part of who I am.

So, Robin, here's me inviting you in whatever way you can to be by my side and in my heart. Now and for ever. I remember our vows at our wedding when we said more or less the same thing:

> *This ring is a symbol of my eternal love for you.*
> *From this day forward you shall never walk alone.*
> *My heart will be your shelter.*
> *My arms will be your home.*

It was, you won't, it is and they are. Always.

Living on in us...

Every time I start thinking this grief thing is so hard to get through, I remind myself that nothing will ever be as tough or heartbreaking as watching the one you love leave the planet when there's *nothing* you can do about it. It must be the hardest, *hardest* thing to see someone you love suffering and nothing in my life could ever be as daunting or haunting as that again.

That should make me feel better, and it does in a way.

What sustains me is believing that he's 'gone home' and, wherever that is, he's not suffering any more. And that whatever it was in him that made us all love him so much is still here in me and in every one of us who loved him. We still carry that part of him in us, in our hearts and in our minds, and that part will live on in us always.

So although he may physically be gone he's still very much here with us, with all of us. And although we must get through this really tough time, we know we've had the joy of having had him in our lives. I hold on to that...

The space between...

I linger in that place between sleep and wakefulness, that delicious space between the two when you're not quite awake yet; or when you're closing your eyes to meditate and for a moment you allow your eyes to hover so you're not quite eyes closed or eyes open, somewhere between the two; that different space, the space between – a calm and peaceful place.

I love those moments. They're a break in time where anything seems possible. Before harsh reality kicks its way back in. I'd stay there for ever if I could.

And here, sitting by the wishbone tree, my mind wanders on. I wonder whether perhaps it feels the same in the space between life and death – most of us don't know about that yet. Maybe, hopefully, it's one of those delicious spaces between two realities. Perhaps it's a good place to be, a stressless space, an intriguing transition between now and then. Or even just a space to finally rest. I guess we'll all know soon...

3-minute mini med...

I've had a few better days since coming back from a weekend meditation retreat. It's a wonder that I went at all, even though it was only three nights. It's been hard for me to leave home for any length of time this year to the point I wondered if I was getting agoraphobic. I wasn't, fortunately. But home is the nest, the sanctuary, my safe space in this ocean of turmoil that grief creates.

But I really felt I needed to get back into my meditation practice and also take time to feel comfortable with myself again.

I hoped through meditation I could 'come back home' to me and find some peace.

Enough to say it was scary at first being somewhere new without the comfort blanket of being home, but it went well and I settled in with the group and the gorgeous surroundings surprisingly easily. Big thanks to all concerned.

So now I'm back and having a better day today, I'm up at the wishbone tree, remembering a 3-minute meditation I learned. It's sometimes known as AGE – Acknowledge, Gather and Expand – and it really helps when I'm feeling scattered and need grounding. It's all about focusing on the breath and here's my memory of how it goes:

Acknowledge the current situation,
Gather the breath and resources,
Expand awareness from the breath into the whole body, and then beyond.

In itself it's been brilliant to take just a few minutes to feel centred and strengthened. But I've also adapted it slightly so that my heart and breath connect with all those who love and support me. I also connect to the sun and the earth, and then gather all that love and light in my heart, like lighting a flame that warms, inspires and strengthens. It feels pretty powerful, especially when I've been feeling crap or vulnerable.

I can then expand that light energy from my heart, the sun and the earth, to fill my whole being, flowing right down to my fingers and my toes, and then expanding around me and across the countryside to fill the world with love and light, healing both me and the earth.

All in all, a pretty good few minutes...

Wise words...
Walking through the wet autumn grass, sometimes words just

come, like someone is telling me something. This came today as I was leaving the hill. 'Love and peace is in your own making. Don't look *for*, look *at*...'

So perhaps I shouldn't spend so much time searching for answers to all these things 'out there' and should take more time to be still and listen. Maybe I might find more of my own kind of peace *inside*. It's good to think so and I'm sure regular meditation will help.

I went back the next day and as I was walking towards the wishbone tree thinking of Robin, I'm sure I heard or *felt* him say: 'I love you. I always did. Be happy.'

How good is that...

A boxful of magic...

I came across a box of old photographs in the loft today. Robin's earlier life in a shoebox. He looks so young, so alive, so fresh, so skinny, so at-the-start-of-it-all. Exotic places, beautiful people, happy smiles, people and events he told me about, there in the flesh. All those years before we met, everything that made him into the man I loved.

I've picked out the pix with him in so that I can take them out sometime later on, sitting by the fire with a glass of wine on a winter's evening, imagining his younger self. It'll take my mind off the later years and his illness, put everything into perspective, help me see him as a whole, complete person. Not just my Robin, but *our* Robin, all of us who loved him.

It's lovely as it's given me a rounder, bigger picture of the man I married, instinctively and without question. The whole Robin and not just the part I knew and loved. It's good, but it makes me miss him more...

Is it possible...

... that we love people *even* more when they're no longer there? Or is it just that we love them most when we finally see the bigger picture and it's too late to tell them? That'd be right. Great eh – instead of bearing up, dealing with the grief and trying to relocate all that love that now has nowhere to go, it just goes on growing. And growing.

The thing is, I've now seen and heard so much more about the 'him' he was before he was the 'him' I knew, there's even more of him to love. Hmm…

Is there love after death?

We often wonder about life after death – possibilities, probabilities, certainties, uncertainties, downright denials. But love after death? Anyone who's been where I am now and has lost someone they love knows that answer without the slightest hesitation. Yes, yes and yes again. Love goes way beyond the physical, it affects us in ways we barely fathom until it's gone – there's no doubt it lives on after death.

As for me, it's still often hard to come to terms with the fact I'll never see him again – not in the easy everyday sense of just being there anyway. My brain knows well enough, but my heart's not so willing to go that last step. He's there in my heart and will remain so as long as I have one. I loved his beautiful physicality, but even more than that I loved his sparkle and spirit and his easy way of being. So, although I may not see him physically anymore, I do carry that sparkle and special way of being inside me. It's both strengthening and comforting, and it means he's always with me. Even though my brain occasionally points out he's not…

Ebbing and flowing…

During this year since Robin's gone and sitting here by the wishbone tree, I feel I've been both resting and bewildered. I'm allowing the cavernous loss to flow in and out of me, watching the waves come and go, trying to stay afloat and not get sucked down into the darkest depths of that scary ocean.

I'm beginning to trust my little boat a bit more. The shore's not always so far off and my survival muscles are ready to row hard if I feel the swell taking me off. It's hopeful...

Feathers and butterflies...

Late afternoon at the wishbone tree with the glowing autumn sunlight and just as I arrived here a beautiful butterfly flew towards me and nestled on the branch beside my head. It was as unexpected as it was unusual. I had to smile. A 'butterfly moment' to add to all those 'white feather moments' I've been noticing all year. Just going out for walks with Freya or without, when thinking of Robin or how I'll survive all this, I'd see a feather on the ground like some sort of sign. Perhaps the 'I'm still here' he used to say every morning. It makes me smile as I thank the bird it came from.

And then today, after the butterfly, two buzzards flew by and circled overhead before heading out across the valley into the late sunlight. Magic moments.

The kiss...

A grey day on the hill today when I arrived. Then as I walked through the wet grass, the clouds parted and revealed a white cross chalked over the clear blue sky. Aeroplanes long gone, or noughts and crosses, or perhaps a kiss. Anything that makes me smile these days is a bit of a bonus...

Losing the bedrock...

Our wedding anniversary, alone. How quickly the ground can swallow you up. And just when you think you're doing okay considering. Okay, maybe it's not surprising I was suddenly in bits and floundering down that deep dark hole again but, believe it or not, it was a surprise to me. I've been saying all year, unusually perhaps, that these 'special' days haven't been any worse than any others because honestly every day has been a challenge. But here I was in instant despair, thrust brutally back to square one. All those 'life lessons' had apparently passed me by and I was just where I was months ago.

I tried to meditate with tears streaming down my face and then heard the words, 'I loved you then, I love you still, I always did and I always will.' Was it me to him? Or him to me? I don't know. In a way it didn't matter. We just loved each other and that was it.

I knew he was the bedrock on which I'd built my life – precious, loving, joyous and secure – and now here I was teetering about in the mud. I realised how deeply he'd slipped into my psyche and my whole being. It wasn't just the flush of love stuff you get when you're young and new to it all, it was also deep and lovely and flourishing and gorgeous in every way. I miss that *so* much.

I'll try to find solid ground again and hopefully I'll feel less like a leaky boat on a deep ocean, but I'll always miss having him by my side. I can imagine and pretend and visualise, but it'll never be the same. 'I loved you then, I love you still, I always did and I always will.' I don't care who said it. It's so true…

Building 'building blocks'…

Again, the wishbone tree has worked its magic. As I sat looking out across the valley, Freya by my side, the ground just looked firmer and the sky more clear. I was back on solid earth, away from the black hole and deep ocean, for a while at least. I've been doing some exercise and meditation before taking Freya out in the mornings and they've become the 'building blocks' of my day. I do them as soon as I get up, before I've had a chance to consider I don't have the time (or the inclination).

The difference to my day has been huge. The solid foundation I've lost with Robin is slowly being replaced by some sort of 'floating mechanism' (like wearing armbands when you're learning to swim?) that makes me feel stronger, and a bit more able get on and do things. I won't overstate this – it's a building block not a replacement, but it's helping in its small, step-by-step way. And at the moment that's great – for me, anything is better than nothing...

Mixed metaphors...

Black holes, deep oceans, solid ground – it's easy to get caught up in the mixed images that float into your mind when you're grieving and your brain is mostly out to lunch. You can only go by how things feel to you at the time.

These images help me, though, because if I'm adrift on an ocean I can see I need a decent boat and some strong oars. Or if I'm down a deep hole, I can see I have to find a way to clamber back out. Each problem brings its own solution. However hard.

If only grief could be so easily cured. For me the hole in my life can only be filled by Robin returning as if none of this ever happened. I may be fanciful but even I can't see that happening, sadly. I have a Robin-shaped hole in my life. So going with it and getting on with it for the life I have left is the only way forward. I know that, but I haven't quite worked out how yet. Maybe it'll come to me in a dream or meditation or daydream. Watch this space...

The heart of it all is love...

It's love that lights the flame of life. It really is. It came to me at the wishbone tree. Whatever else goes on in life, love is what lights us up – from conception to enlightenment, from birth through to death, during everything in between and most likely thereafter, it's love that lights our way. I don't mean this in any special religious way – I've always been open-minded and spiritual, but I'm not tied to any specific religious path.

I often imagine the light as a flame, starting small when first lit and then growing in warmth and power and intensity the more it's nurtured. Love, like oxygen, can make that flame burn as brightly as you want. Any time. Anywhere. (And it saves on heating...)

Which is why, I think, grief so often makes me feel cold and isolated. No warmth, no flame, no love. I meditate on this sometimes and can often create a flame running through my body, bringing light and strength where there was none before. It's a small thing, but these days everything helps...

Wow, I never noticed that before...

Standing by the wishbone tree in its winter mode, more noticeable and stark in the icy sunshine, I've just realised that it itself is broken. And surviving. How come I never noticed that before? It's why, of course, it's the 'wishbone' tree at all, because one of the main branches has fallen and is cradled over the lower trunk. How stupid am I??? Looking without seeing, I expect I do it all the time.

So we're both broken, it and me. But if the wishbone tree can stand proud and straight at the top of the hill, where it no doubt gets buffeted and bullied by wind and rain, and patiently puts up with a mad widow every few days, then that's another lesson it's taught me. Just get on and do it. Live while you can, make the most of each moment, take what comes and carry on.

Trees can't run away or yearn for the past or wish it was all different. (I don't think...) And neither will I. This is bloody hard and it's up and down, but it's my life and I've got to live it. Well, maybe not quite yet, but I will. Soon...

Dancing in the rain...

It's that time of year again – Christmas, when everyone is busy, shopping, partying and planning festivities with partners, family and friends. Or that's how it seems from the distant planet I now inhabit. I suspect some of them, like me, may just be pretending to be normal. I'm not a great actress so putting on a brave face isn't my best role. I'd rather just do it all quietly and gently in my own time in my own way.

Not allowed. 'You *can't* be on your own. Come to us – we'll cheer you up, you'll have a great time…' It's kind and thoughtful. But I am all right. I'm not totally sinking under the pressure. Usually. And I like my own company.

But then I remember all the small things we used to do together: decorations, writing cards (my writing was never readable enough to be entrusted with addressing envelopes), planning and making fantastic food, and tracking down lovely pressies. Aah yes. That was then and this is now.

I'm putting off doing the cards and they're sitting beside me in a neat pile, waiting patiently to be written. I don't know what to say, so maybe I'll just sign my name. But that looks a bit lost floating in a big white space on its own without at least a few words added. Oh here we go slipping down the 'poor little old me on my ownsome' slope. Yuk. Get a grip.

So I put the whole thing off for another day, make a cup of tea and end up writing this instead. Whoever said, 'Life isn't about waiting for the storm to pass, it's about learning to dance in the rain,' didn't live in festive December Dorset. For somewhere so far out in the sticks, it's a mass of activity at Christmas. Special lunches, shows, parties, carol singing, drinks and festive fun. The inspiring thing is that many of the locals *are* out there 'dancing in the rain', in spite of their own various problems (health and otherwise) and daily issues. It's a lesson to us all, especially me, so enough of the bah humbug, let's get out the mulled wine and go carolling…

Bottling out - again…

Okay, so I didn't go carolling. Though I did hand out the mulled wine (and tasted it too, of course). All that festive fun when I'd rather stay in by the fire and nurse my broken heart seemed just a step too far this year. The wishbone tree generously agreed when I admitted my failing the next day. 'Go with the flow. Forgive yourself everything and just do what feels right.'

So I did, and I am. The cards got written and posted. It's okay to be sad. I'm not wallowing, I'm just being quiet while Christmas whistles through. It's okay. It's fine. I love a dead man. Sounds weird put like that, but many of us do. It's true for so many people. Especially at this time of year.

I don't feel sorry for myself, it's just the way it is. He's there and I'm here. Nothing I can do about it for now. I'm cheering myself up with mince pies. Why are they only available at Christmas? They're *so* moreish. Off to get another one...

Trying to be normal...

What's normal? It felt like it'd be a safe space when a neighbour asked a few of us in for Christmas drinks and nibbles – not far to go and easy to rush home if necessary. Lovely people, what could go wrong?

The elephant in the room was the huge space left by Robin not being there. Maybe it was only me who noticed it. I tried to be normal and join in – hard, hard, hard. Left after an hour. Why can't I do this. The normal things. I still miss him so much. Eleven months on and I'm hardly moving forward at all...

Half a life...

When you're so close as a couple it's hard to know how much you become entangled with your partner. If I often feel I'm living half a life or am half a person since he left, could it be because he's taken part of me with him? Of course we were separate entities with different interests and rich lives, but if our spirits/ energy/souls merged into each other, what happens when part of that moves on? Maybe, wherever he is now and in whatever form, he misses me like I miss him. Part of *me* may be missing because it's with him, and part of *him* may be missing because it's still here. (There's his favourite phrase again: 'I'm still here.')

So what if this dying business is an ongoing process of slowly separating our more subtle energies even long after the physical separation from the earthly body has taken place? Perhaps that's why it's still so painful for so long for those of us left behind. And who knows what it's like for those who've gone…

Untying the ties…

When Robin and I first met we instantly felt comfortable together, almost like we'd known each other before or for ever. We were very close but we were never the same. It was our differences that made us endlessly intrigued and interested in each other. We just clicked and quickly became compatible, snapping together like two final pieces in a puzzle.

It was so easy to be with each other, almost hard to see how we'd spent so much time in our lives apart, and yet it was that 'apartness' that made it so good when we were together because we had such a lot to bring to the party.

We were different people and yet I think our spirits became so enmeshed because we were very comfortable in our own company. It was that which bonded us and brought us together – all those subtle levels and layers. It feels like those are the ones that take the longest to untangle and let go of when the physical body is no longer there, when death occurs.

If all that's true, this process of grieving will obviously go on much longer because, although the physical separation has happened, the emotional, energetic, spiritual or soul links are still very much there. In our way, part of him became part of me and part of me became part of him.

I guess the benefit of that is that he'll always go on living in me and in all of us who loved him. I'll cherish and love him always. And sometime in the future when the wounds of separation are a little less raw, I'll hold the memory of our lives together as a warm glowing ember that brings me comfort and joy. One day…

Going on without me…

I had strange dreams last night and woke anxiously repeating

Robin's name over and over again. I was calling to him as if he was leaving and going somewhere without me, somewhere I couldn't follow. I heard myself say, 'Take me with you, take me with you!' immediately followed by a panicky, 'No not yet, there's too much to do, I have to sort it all out. I can't, I'm not ready.' The rest of the night was fearful and anxious as I blearily tried to make sense of it all.

Where did that come from? It hit me completely out of the blue. It was six days before the first anniversary of his death (that unreal word again). I began wondering if our recently departed are only able to stay close to us for that first year and then have to move on and go away for ever. Panic set in again as, although I obviously haven't physically seen him in nearly a year, I've always felt him around and recognised his hand in the various ways I deal with daily tasks without him.

This is all so hard. I thought maybe I was going mad. But, as they say, life goes on. So even though tired and emotional, I had to get up and carry on as I had people coming to stay. I would have loved a therapeutic 'duvet day' – I've always fancied one of those, but never seem to have the time. Why is there always so much to do? Perhaps I should be more organised, then maybe I'd be more on top of it all.

But what did that dream mean? Was I with him and losing him all over again? Or was it just my subconscious playing tricks because the one-year anniversary was so close? Who knows. It helps me to write it down and try to understand what's going on in my head.

Hmm, that'll be the day…

The dreaded deadline…

It's strange how we create false deadlines in life as if something miraculous or terrible is going to happen on a particular day or a particular time. I then realised I'd been building myself up to this momentous occasion – one year since Robin left. I must have subconsciously given myself a year to grieve, let go, be mad, weep, stay home etc before people (I thought) most likely expected me to get a grip, be normal, get on with it, move on.

I suspect we do it all the time – put our lives on hold because they're dependant on something else happening first. We say, 'I can't do that until…', or 'I'll do that later when…' Real deadlines are one thing. Made up random future dates simply screw us up.

And special dates, such as anniversaries, bring their own traumas. They are, after all, just days in a diary and in themselves should hold no fear. But, of course, they do. Because that's how we work. We're conditioned by time.

New year is a great example. Why should our lives change in an instant at midnight on the 31 December? Why is it so significant that yesterday was 2017 and today is 2018? (Except, of course, for me Robin was alive for a week and a half in 2017 and now isn't in 2018.)

After the event, it turned out I was dreading 8.30am on Tuesday 9 January because that was the moment he died. I felt that momentous instant should be marked somehow (but had no idea how) and his sister Lynne was here with me. We lit a candle and got out some photos. We cried and laughed at some of the memories. And after that we simply had breakfast and went up to the wishbone tree.

It was a grey and misty morning and you could barely see anything beyond the brow of the hill. Strangely, it felt almost cosy – a small world contained and covered in mist.

The wishbone tree wended its magic and I was feeling lighter and more peaceful as we tramped through muddy grass back across the hill. The dreaded deadline of 8.30am had come and gone and it felt like a weight had been lifted.

On that slightly more positive note, it's on into the new year…

Life's rhythms…

It's feeling right to create a new rhythm to my life. My grief and sadness is still here and will never go away, I know that, but I can try to live with it better. So instead of avoiding committing to regular dates in the diary or making far distant arrangements, it now feels a little safer to make a few gentle plans. There will always be the proviso that I can bottle out or change my mind on the day if necessary and that I won't push myself when I'm not ready, but even having the intention is a start.

This new rhythm feels like a positive step. I've been going so much with the ebb and flow of grief, I've lost the habit of going out and doing things. Maybe it's time to take stock.

I'm starting with going back to my Tai Chi – always a gentle and restoring way for me to feel better about life. And I'll play more piano and probably end up writing endless sad songs, like I did in my love-strewn youth, but it'll be fun. Music is so therapeutic.

Taking it slowly, that's the key. Not too much, not too often. I like my own company and have never been a party animal, so just a bit at a time will be fine. For now.

Here I go, travelling hopefully again…

Getting used to getting used to it…

I've been feeling a strange calm since January passed. Am I just getting used to living without Robin? *No*, something screams inside me, temporarily breaking the silence. Okay I know I can never expect that – how could I ever get used to being without him or not having him around. Or wishing he was here beside me. But maybe I'm just getting more used to bearing the pain.

For me, my grief is now about learning how to carry the heavy loss – I know it's not going to go away, but I reckon that learning to accommodate it and carry it around without toppling over is the key. I'll just carry on carrying on and hope it'll get easier, like training to lift heavy weights. It's not easy but, after a while, I hope it'll become slightly less heavy and overwhelming. I'll be used to carrying the weight and won't be quite so crippled by it.

Tai chi and meditation are proving to be a good combination to help me find some calm and balance. That and the wishbone tree, of course. I'm discovering what the important things are for me in the life I have left. I have to live for both of us now. I can't waste this time.

I heard recently that former US President Obama was once asked if he had a 'bucket list' of things to do now he was no longer in office. He apparently said no but he had something that rhymes with it. Ha, ha, me too. It made me smile...

I hope this calm lasts. At least for a while. And when the silent storm inside rages up again, I'll talk to myself like a mother talks to their child, I'll go see the wishbone tree, maybe take the odd duvet day.

Life throws these things at us and through it all I've discovered that love has been my greatest joy and toughest teacher. I love a dead man. But, ups and downs aside, I will survive.

Tales From the Wishbone Tree

Part Three

What Helped Me

What can you do or say to someone who's lost their life's love? I didn't know what I needed, I barely knew where I was. And then we're all so unique, it can seem hard to know what's best. With my new-found (but unwanted) experience, I can now see that some things work better than others – for me, anyway. I have to say this is purely my personal view and not a definitive list of dos and don'ts for grieving folks...

1) First and foremost, **people** helped me. Not that I wanted them to and not that I thought I needed them to then, but each in their own unique ways they all did. Their patience and understanding especially.

2) I couldn't take seeing many people at once. **One to one** was the easiest for me to deal with at first. It created an instant balance (okay, I'm a Libran...) and I didn't feel I had to entertain them or play the perfect host. As soon as others were involved I found it far harder to cope and found myself getting stressed and anxious. Somewhere in my mind I felt I should be my usual host-like self and feed and take care of them. The stress it led to made me irritable and unable to relax.

I've profusely apologised to those I may have offended, and I hope they realise that because my emotions were so close to the surface, the slightest thing just set me off. My consequential guilt at *not* being able to be my usual coping self stopped me from sleeping which, of course, just made it all worse. Sorry, folks. It's just the way it was.

3) Having **someone to listen** to me also helped beyond measure. It's hard for any of us to know how to deal with someone going through life-changing loss. What could anyone say to make it any better? And of course everyone worries about saying the wrong things, so often don't say anything at all. Actually, that's fine by me. I'd rather have someone say, 'I'm really sorry I don't know what to say, but I'm always here for you – do you fancy a glass of wine/cup of tea/beans on toast etc...'

Listening was the best thing. Those who gave me the chance to 'let it all out' and talk about Robin (I wanted to talk about him and keep him in the conversation the whole time) were worth their weight in gold. It's always so tempting for people to sympathise and say, 'I know just how you feel,' and launch into their own story about somebody's best friend's sister's neighbour's cousin's boyfriend's mother who has just been through exactly the same thing and how awful it all was... I'm sure I've done it myself many times, but believe me it doesn't help when all you want to do is scream.

4) I also know now it's better if people take time to **manage their own feelings first** before immediately rushing up to someone who's grieving. To be honest I was so out of it and so tired by all that had been and was now going on, it was really tough dealing with other people's reactions, too. I just needed time and quiet for the reality to settle into my poor brain, never mind my breaking heart.

5) 'How are you?' is another phrase I found fraught with difficulty. Again, I know I've asked it myself many times just because that's what we do without thinking when we meet someone we know. On the receiving end and having just lost my beloved husband, I now see how hard it is to offer a true reply. I could have said a quick, 'Fine, thank you,' and moved swiftly on, but they'd have known that was rubbish. I got into saying, 'Oh up and down, you know,' and shrugged my shoulders, usually trying to hold back the tears.

I read somewhere that the best way to do it if you want to know how a bereaved person is, is to **ask how they're doing** *today* on the understanding that every day feels different and all you can be expected to do is deal with 24 hours at a time. Seems to make sense and I think I like it better.

6) People offering **practical help and support** were also brilliant. Lots of people say, 'Let me know if I can help in any way,' and that's great but I could never think of how or what or when. But if someone said, 'Can I get you some shopping today?' or 'Can I walk the dog for you?' or 'How about I make some supper tonight,' I felt like falling on them in gratitude. It's the daily chores I just wasn't in the mood to do, especially if it involved going out in public. I felt so much safer at home where meltdowns could take place in private...

7) I'm lucky to have a **loving family** who were totally 'there' for us from the word go. Our sisters and their families all live in different parts of the country but regularly came down when Robin was up to it, and texted, emailed and phoned when he wasn't. Their love and care held us together and kept our little boat afloat. Since Robin has gone, they've still kept in close touch and we go on supporting each other. Couldn't do it without them.

8) **Good friends and neighbours** have also been a godsend. We live in what must be about the most caring village in Dorset. Help and sympathy is always at hand and they've been beyond great. People feel free to drop by and are very welcome, it's lovely to see them, but they also understand the times I need to be alone and just can't come to all the village events.

9) We're all different and I knew from the start **I had to go through this my way**, to honour my love for Robin and to survive somehow as a whole human being.

We had the Kahlil Gibran 'let there be space in your love'

poem about marriage from *The Prophet* at our wedding. It suddenly seems even more appropriate now we're separated.

You were born together, and together you shall be for evermore.
You shall be together when the white wings of death scatter your
days.
Aye, you shall be together even in the silent memory of God.
But let there be spaces in your togetherness,
And let the winds of the heavens dance between you.

Love one another but make not a bond of love:
Let it rather be a moving sea between the shores of your souls.
Fill each other's cup but drink not from one cup.
Give one another of your bread but eat not from the same loaf.
Sing and dance together and be joyous, but let each one of you be
alone,
Even as the strings of a lute are alone though they quiver with the
same music.

Give your hearts, but not into each other's keeping.
For only the hand of Life can contain your hearts.
And stand together, yet not too near together:
For the pillars of the temple stand apart,
And the oak tree and the cypress grow not in each other's shadow.

I love that poem and I loved Robin. He will always be with me, safely stored in my heart as I face life's new challenges and become this strange new person called 'me'.

What else helped?

10) Our lovely dog Freya who needs feeding twice a day, who needs me to play with her, who drags me out for walks, who shows me that the beauty of nature and the countryside lives on in spite of what happens to us, who leans against me on the sofa, who looks up at me with deep understanding eyes.

11) And of course **the wishbone tree**. It's a place I feel nurtures and nourishes me. It's a place where I feel free, where I listen and watch. It's a place of boundless views over beautiful west Dorset, infinite skies and endless sea. It's my place of solace and connection. My heart space. I suspect we all need places like that, whether in cities or countryside, somewhere we feel whole, somewhere that moves and restores our soul.

12) Finally? **Hugs**. I needed those in abundance, though not at first when I was finding it so hard to keep my body and soul together. Hugs are the glue of love. More? Oh go on then…

Things I've Learned

Lots. And lots. And more lots. I could have read it all in books. I could have gone on courses. But someone 'upstairs' in their wisdom thought this was the best way to get some of these smidgens of wisdom into my poor brain – and heart.

No I don't recommend becoming a widow. Or widower. Or going through any kind of loss. I'd give anything to have it back the way it was. The what ifs. The if onlys. The why us.

But after a while you realise that's just the way it is. Birth and death happen all the time to everyone on this planet. It's hardly unusual. But, sadly, that doesn't make it any easier for any of us.

I've lost count of the number of people I know who are making (and working through) their 'bucket lists'. The greatest lesson? Do it NOW. Say it NOW. Don't wait till it's too late. But then I didn't need to go through all this to know that. It's blindingly obvious that technically we're dying from the moment we're born.

Anyway, enough of the gloomy stuff. What else have I learned?

Love more, whinge less.

Be kind and compassionate.

Be wise (experience) as well as knowledgeable (learning).

Be nice.

Tell people you love that you love them.

Go to sleep every night thinking that if you died

tonight, you'd have no regrets (apart from dying too soon...).

As well as those general-but-oh-so-true clichés, there are other things I have learned.

Grief is a great teacher if we sit with it and listen. There's no point in avoiding it or running away from it because it'll only pop up and bite you later on. If you love someone, losing them is going to hurt. And grief is the price we pay for love. When it's not destroying you, it's making you stronger. In all sorts of ways. It's hard to see at first, but little by little we start to learn to live in our new world. Slowly, slowly – it takes time.

Losing the man I love has broken me. But in trying to put the pieces back together it's also made me more understanding, I think. This will be an ongoing process, but I'm not so quick to jump to conclusions or judge others any more. I know I don't know what it's like to stand in their shoes and so there's no point presuming I might know how they really feel or what's right for them.

Being less judgemental is a great lesson. The kindest and most helpful people were often the most unexpected. I'm lucky that everyone has been lovely but some went beyond beyond. It's humbled me to see how kind and understanding people can be without wanting anything in return. It reminds me of a time long ago when I was sitting shelling broad beans and suddenly discovered that it was the imperfect gnarled pods that often held the gorgeous succulent beans, whereas the plump green pods only had blackened or tiny beans. I learned a lesson there – the 'don't judge a book by its cover' sort of daily wisdom.

I've learned, too, you don't always get what you want and I'm trying hard to let go of expectations. Some things are just outside our control and there's nothing we can do about it. It's taken me a while to reconcile that, but I'm learning to stand back and trust, and go with the flow a little more.

I also know that gratitude is better than resentment. It's easy to get angry about the stuff that happens to us and to those we love. But when we're already distraught and vulnerable, anger takes a lot of energy. I decided it was better to be glad and thankful for what I'd had with Robin rather than resentful that it had been taken away from me.

I learned that the glass half full and half empty syndrome was a waste of time – why worry about which side of the glass you're on when anyone can see it simply needs refilling. (Sometimes we just get hung up on the wrong things?)

People living with a terminal disease still need space to live and be themselves for whatever time they have left. They are still the same person inside, even when they're ill, and deserve the same respect and choices as they did before. There were a few things that I may now, in hindsight, have done a little differently, though my love for my Robin never wavered. And, thankfully, he knew that.

I'm sure I now value my family and friends much more. Until you're really tested, it's easy to take people for granted. My lovely sisters and sister-in-law, cousins and their families were brilliant even though we don't usually see each other all that often as we live in different parts of the country. But when they heard Robin's news, they were totally 'there' for us from the word go. As Robin and I had no kids of our own, they all became a beautiful focus of care and consideration. These things have certainly made us closer. We support each other in our loss because it affects us all, not just me. Especially, of course, Robin's sister and her amazing family.

Friends likewise – they say you learn in a crisis who your real friends are. I reckoned I knew before, but I certainly know now who loves and understands us. They were sensitive enough to leave us alone when we needed space, and to be there for me later when I needed them. And fortunately still are...

I've discovered how important living in a caring community

is. Neighbours – new and old, what would we have done without them? Soups, casseroles, cakes, summer puddings (Robin's favourite), mousses and ice creams turned up at the door in the hands of our lovely friends from the village. Robin's best buddies regularly popped by to see how he was and cheer him up, or just to sit with him quietly. Other neighbours helped by dogsitting or walking Freya if I had to be at the hospital or couldn't leave Robin. They sorted the daily things so I didn't have to worry and gave me a hug when I looked in need of support.

And from those in further reaches of the country, emails, letters and cards kept arriving – better for me in many ways than people phoning as I wasn't always able to speak about what was going on, especially after Robin had gone. When things were bad, it was lovely to feel the support without worrying about the need to respond immediately.

I've learned to be more open and honest about things, too. I suppose when you're close to the edge, there's no point in fudging the issues or being unclear about what you do or don't need. As someone who prefers calm and balance, I used to spend a lot of time trying to keep the peace and consider everything from everyone's point of view. More recently, life's literally been too short for all that and I now appreciate that honesty is the best policy. I'm still learning to 'speak my truth' from my heart rather than my red-hot head, and it may take a while, but I hope I'm getting there slowly.

Favourite Quotes and Sayings

I have always loved playing with words and so often wish I had just the right thing to say. Fortunately, many other people have already expressed these things so much better than me. Here are some of my favourite quotes that I've found helpful during these precarious times (starting with someone special)...

The greatest gift any human has is to love and be loved.
Robin Eaton

Goodbyes are only for those who love with their eyes.
Because for those who love with heart and soul, there is no such thing as separation.
Rumi

Sometimes it's okay if the only thing you did today was breathe.
Yumi Sakugawa

I am not this hair
I am not this skin
I am the soul that lives within...
Rumi

Grief is really just love. It's all the love you want to give, but cannot. All that unspent love gathers up in the corners of your eyes, the lump in your throat, and in that hollow part of your chest. Grief is just love with no place to go.
Jamie Anderson

People who need help sometimes look a lot like people who don't need help.
Glennon Doyle Melton

Sometimes when things are falling apart, they may actually be falling into place...
Unknown

There are some who bring a light so great into the world that even after they have gone the light remains.
Unknown

If there ever comes a day when we can't be together, keep me in your heart and I'll stay there for ever.
Winnie the Pooh

Grief, I've learned, is just another name for Love; they are here, together, and we can be with them both.
Jen, author of Aim Happy

It's hard to forget someone who gave you so much to remember.
Unknown

But in all of the sadness, when you're feeling that your heart is empty, and lacking, you've got to remember that grief isn't the absence of love. Grief is the proof that love is still there.
Tessa Shaffer, Heaven Has No Regrets

We never lose our loved ones. They accompany us; they don't disappear from our lives. We are merely in different rooms.
Paulo Coelho, Aleph

I want to be thoroughly used up when I die, for the harder

I work, the more I live. I rejoice in life for its own sake. Life is no brief candle to me; it is a sort of splendid torch which I have got hold of for the moment, and I want to make it burn as brightly as possible before handing it on to future generations.
George Bernard Shaw

What the caterpillar calls the end of the world, the master calls a butterfly.
Richard Bach

Absence, the highest form of presence.
James Joyce

Perhaps they are not stars in the sky but rather openings where our loved ones shine down to let us know they are happy.
Eskimo saying

Courage doesn't always roar. Sometimes courage is the little voice at the end of the day that says I'll try again tomorrow.
Mary Ann Radmacher

When one person is missing the whole world seems empty.
Pat Schwiebert

Life isn't about waiting for the storm to pass. It's about learning to dance in the rain.
Vivian Greene

The timeless in you is aware of life's timelessness. And knows that yesterday is but today's memory and tomorrow is today's dream.
Kahlil Gibran, The Prophet

Yesterday I was clever, so I wanted to change the world. Today I am wise, so I am changing myself.
Rumi

Travel through life with two sticks to support you. One is service and the other is kindness.
Unknown

If it weren't for the last minute, nothing would ever get done.
Rita Mae Brown

If you can't listen, you can't talk.
Unknown

When the power of love overcomes the love of power the world will know peace.
Jimi Hendrix

Do not look back on happiness or dream of it in the future. You are only sure of today; do not let yourself be cheated of it.
Henry Ward Beecher

Man cannot discover new oceans unless he has the courage to lose sight of the shore.
André Gide

Do not dwell in the past, do not dream of the future, concentrate the mind on the present moment.
Buddha

Today's mighty oak is just yesterday's nut that held its ground.
David Icke

Over every mountain there is a path, though you may not see it from the valley.
Theodore Roethke

In life there are only a small number of people whom we choose to keep in our hearts. Over the years a lot come in and go out: lovers, family, and friends. Some hang around for a while, and some want to stay even after we have ordered them to leave. But only a handful, no more than two handfuls if you're very lucky, are welcome for ever.
Jonathan Carroll

Life's journey is not to arrive at the grave safely in a perfectly preserved body, but rather to skid in sideways, totally worn out, shouting, 'Holy shit, what a ride!'
Mavis Leyrer

In the depth of winter, I finally learned that within me there lay an invincible summer.
Albert Camus

People are like stained glass windows: they sparkle and shine when the sun is out, but when the darkness sets in, their true beauty is revealed only if there is a light within.
Elisabeth Kübler-Ross

To be beautiful means to be yourself. You don't need to be accepted by others. You need to accept yourself.
Thich Nhat Hanh

Happiness depends on inner peace, which depends on warm-heartedness. There's no room for anger, jealousy or insecurity. A calm mind and self-confidence are the basis for peaceful relations with others. Scientists have observed

that constant anger and fear eat away at our immune system, whereas a calm mind strengthens it. Changing the world for the better begins with individuals creating inner peace within themselves.
Dalai Lama

People who shine from within don't need the spotlight.
Unknown

Try to be a rainbow in someone's cloud.
Maya Angelou

Sometimes the wrong choices bring us to the right places.
Unknown

All the wonders you seek are within yourself.
Sir Thomas Browne

Happiness is the absence of striving for happiness.
Chuang-Tse

If the doors of perception were cleansed, everything would appear to man as it is. Infinite. For man has closed himself up, till he sees all things thro' narrow chinks of his cavern.
William Blake

He who would be what he ought to be, must stop being what he is.
Medieval Christian mystic Meister Eckhart

Some people think it's holding on that makes one strong – sometimes it's letting go.
Unknown

Tension is who you think you should be. Relaxation is who you are.
Chinese proverb

Do the best you can, from where you are, with what you have, now.
African-American proverb

Lamps are different. Light is the same.
Unknown

Because suffering is impermanent, that is why we can transform it.
Because happiness is impermanent, that is why we have to nourish it.
Thich Nhat Hanh

Some people come into your life as blessings. Others come into your life as lessons.
Mother Teresa

It is never too late to be what you might have been.
George Eliot

Just when the caterpillar thought the world was over, it became a butterfly...
Unknown

We're all just walking each other home.
Ram Dass

Eternity can be touched in the present moment, and the cosmos in the palm of your hand.
Thich Nhat Hanh

If you love a flower, don't pick it up.
Because if you pick it up it dies and it ceases to be what you love.
So if you love a flower, let it be.
Love is not about possession.
Love is about appreciation.
Osho

Grief changes shape, but it never ends.
Keanu Reeves

If you live in fear of the future because of what happened in your past, you'll end up losing what you have in the present.
Nishan Panwar

Deep in our hearts your memory is kept, we loved you too deeply to ever forget.
Unknown

Do not go where the path may lead, go instead where there is no path and leave a trail.
Ralph Waldo Emerson

You are not stuck where you are unless you decide to be.
Wayne Dyer

No Mud, No Lotus.
Thich Nhat Hanh

We are all visitors to this time, this place. We are just passing through. Our purpose here is to observe, to learn, to grow, to love... and then we return home.
Aboriginal Proverb

Change the way you look at things and the things you look at change.
Wayne Dyer

Do not let the behaviour of others destroy your inner peace.
Dalai Lama

Every emotion is temporary. Any emotion known to man is a fleeting, impermanent state (even the happy ones). Think of them like waves. Sometimes you can see it coming, other times it catches you by surprise. Some waves are bigger than others; however, by their nature they come and go.
Diane Webb

My wife has recently changed her residency to heaven.
From the film Human

I would not interfere with any creed of yours, or want to appear I have all the cures. There is so much to know, so many things are true. The way my feet must go, may not be right for you. And so I give this spark, of what is light to me, to guide you through the dark but not to tell you what to see.
Unknown

They say the hardest thing in the world is losing someone you love. Someone you grew old with and watched grow everyday. Someone who showed you how to love. It's the worst thing to ever happen to anyone. My wife died unexpectedly. She brought me so much joy. She was my everything. Those 16 years of being her husband taught me how to love unconditionally. We have to stop and be thankful for our spouses. Because, life is very short. Spend time with your spouses. Treat them well. Because, one day, when you look up from your phone, they won't be there anymore. What

I truly learned most of all is, live and love everyday like it's your last. Because, one day, it will be. Take chances and go live life. Tell the ones you love, that you love them everyday. Don't take any moment for granted. Life is worth living.
Liam Neeson

The only true wisdom is in knowing you know nothing.
Socrates

Our task must be to free ourselves by widening our circle of compassion to embrace all living creatures and the whole of nature in its beauty.
Albert Einstein

Three wise women would have asked directions, arrived on time, helped deliver the baby, brought practical gifts, cleaned the stable, made a casserole, and there would be world peace.
Unknown

Afterwords...

I realised when I read all this back, the whole thing seems to be just about Robin and me, and the effect his illness has had on our lives. Okay, guilty as charged. But it's not true, of course. His loss has had a much wider effect than that.

This isn't a burden I carry alone. His leaving the planet has deeply affected all of us who knew and loved him. We all know the world is a poorer place without Robin in it. He left a chasm no one can bridge, a gap no one can fill.

We may get used to our strange new lives without him eventually, but there's no denying the huge hole in our little planet's 'fabric of life'. A stitch is missing in the great tapestry. There's a gap in the ether. It makes you want to scream, 'Come back!' or 'Where have you *gone*?!'

That 'hole' has taught me many things. But these are lessons I would willingly have done without. The price of that particular 'education' was far too high. Peace of mind is priceless. And I miss it.

At the wishbone tree I could shout out: 'Bring me back my inner peace! Bring me back my boring contentedness! Bring me back my fun and joyfulness! Bring me back my Robin! Bring me...'

I don't, though. Why not? Because I *have* the wishbone tree. It's a peaceful, generous, wise old tree and it knows far better than me how to survive life's trials and challenges. So I sit there and listen. And I learn something new every time.

We all need a wishbone tree. The world would be a better place if we all had our own wise old tree to talk to...

Just a final thought...
I'm a different person to the one who started writing this two and a half years ago. I've gained and I've lost.

I think I'm more understanding of others' situations. I know now I'll never have all the answers. From my earlier years as an enthusiastic, busy, coping journalist, through the blossoming era of offering and teaching rewarding natural therapies, to my more recent meditative, appreciative, sometimes struggling widowhood, there's been a vast transition. But, as Robin used to say, I'm still here.

And there's nothing unusual in my story. We all move through life gaining and losing. We all face problems of varying kinds and huge losses along the way. That's all made me the woman I am now, for better and worse.

So take me as you find me, ups and downs, warts and all, sometimes broken and sometimes mended. I am, after all, a recycled human being. We all are. And that's our strength.

I know I've been saying we're all different and respond to life's ups and downs in our own unique ways, and that's true. But I'm also aware how much we're intricately connected. Happiness/sorrow, love/loss, life/death – we all learn soon enough you can't have one without the other. As Buddhist monk Thich Nhat Hanh says, 'No mud, no lotus.' It's brilliantly simple and true.

I'm quite sure, as travellers on our epic journeys, we have many more things in common than those that divide us. I wish us all love, wisdom, peace and good fortune...

It only takes the tiniest light to pierce the darkness.

The tiniest light can grow into the greatest flame.

~ HVE ~

BOOKS

O-BOOKS

SPIRITUALITY

O is a symbol of the world, of oneness and unity; this eye represents knowledge and insight. We publish titles on general spirituality and living a spiritual life. We aim to inform and help you on your own journey in this life.

If you have enjoyed this book, why not tell other readers by posting a review on your preferred book site?

Recent bestsellers from O-Books are:

Heart of Tantric Sex
Diana Richardson
Revealing Eastern secrets of deep love and intimacy to Western couples.
Paperback: 978-1-90381-637-0 ebook: 978-1-84694-637-0

Crystal Prescriptions
The A-Z guide to over 1,200 symptoms and their healing crystals
Judy Hall
The first in the popular series of six books, this handy little guide is packed as tight as a pill-bottle with crystal remedies for ailments.
Paperback: 978-1-90504-740-6 ebook: 978-1-84694-629-5

Take Me To Truth
Undoing the Ego
Nouk Sanchez, Tomas Vieira
The best-selling step-by-step book on shedding the Ego, using the teachings of *A Course In Miracles*.
Paperback: 978-1-84694-050-7 ebook: 978-1-84694-654-7

The 7 Myths about Love...Actually!
The journey from your HEAD to the HEART of your SOUL
Mike George
Smashes all the myths about LOVE.
Paperback: 978-1-84694-288-4 ebook: 978-1-84694-682-0

The Holy Spirit's Interpretation of the New Testament
A course in Understanding and Acceptance
Regina Dawn Akers
Following on from the strength of *A Course In Miracles*, NTI
teaches us how to experience the love and oneness of God.
Paperback: 978-1-84694-085-9 ebook: 978-1-78099-083-5

The Message of A Course In Miracles
A translation of the text in plain language
Elizabeth A. Cronkhite
A translation of *A Course in Miracles* into plain, everyday
language for anyone seeking inner peace. The companion
volume, *Practicing A Course In Miracles*, offers practical lessons
and mentoring.
Paperback: 978-1-84694-319-5 ebook: 978-1-84694-642-4

Rising in Love
My Wild and Crazy Ride to Here and Now, with Amma, the
Hugging Saint
Ram Das Batchelder
Rising in Love conveys an author's extraordinary journey of
spiritual awakening with the Guru, Amma.
Paperback: 978-1-78279-687-9 ebook: 978-1-78279-686-2

Thinker's Guide to God
Peter Vardy
An introduction to key issues in the philosophy of religion.
Paperback: 978-1-90381-622-6

Your Simple Path
Find happiness in every step
Ian Tucker
A guide to helping us reconnect with what is really important
in our lives.
Paperback: 978-1-78279-349-6 ebook: 978-1-78279-348-9

365 Days of Wisdom
Daily Messages To Inspire You Through The Year
Dadi Janki
Daily messages which cool the mind, warm the heart and guide
you along your journey.
Paperback: 978-1-84694-863-3 ebook: 978-1-84694-864-0

Body of Wisdom
Women's Spiritual Power and How it Serves
Hilary Hart
Bringing together the dreams and experiences of women across
the world with today's most visionary spiritual teachers.
Paperback: 978-1-78099-696-7 ebook: 978-1-78099-695-0

Dying to Be Free
From Enforced Secrecy to Near Death to True Transformation
Hannah Robinson
After an unexpected accident and near-death experience,
Hannah Robinson found herself radically transforming her life,
while a remarkable new insight altered her relationship with
her father, a practising Catholic priest.
Paperback: 978-1-78535-254-6 ebook: 978-1-78535-255-3

The Ecology of the Soul
A Manual of Peace, Power and Personal Growth for Real People
in the Real World
Aidan Walker
Balance your own inner Ecology of the Soul to regain your
natural state of peace, power and wellbeing.
Paperback: 978-1-78279-850-7 ebook: 978-1-78279-849-1

Not I, Not other than I
The Life and Teachings of Russel Williams
Steve Taylor, Russel Williams
The miraculous life and inspiring teachings of one of the
World's greatest living Sages.
Paperback: 978-1-78279-729-6 ebook: 978-1-78279-728-9

On the Other Side of Love
A Woman's Unconventional Journey Towards Wisdom
Muriel Maufroy
When life has lost all meaning, what do you do?
Paperback: 978-1-78535-281-2 ebook: 978-1-78535-282-9

Practicing A Course In Miracles
A Translation of the Workbook in Plain Language and With
Mentoring Notes
Elizabeth A. Cronkhite
The practical second and third volumes of The Plain-Language
A Course In Miracles.
Paperback: 978-1-84694-403-1 ebook: 978-1-78099-072-9

Quantum Bliss
The Quantum Mechanics of Happiness, Abundance, and Health
George S. Mentz
Quantum Bliss is the breakthrough summary of success and
spirituality secrets that customers have been waiting for.
Paperback: 978-1-78535-203-4 ebook: 978-1-78535-204-1

The Upside Down Mountain
Mags MacKean
A must-read for anyone weary of chasing success and
happiness – one woman's inspirational journey swapping the
uphill slog for the downhill slope.
Paperback: 978-1-78535-171-6 ebook: 978-1-78535-172-3

Your Personal Tuning Fork
The Endocrine System
Deborah Bates
Discover your body's health secret, the endocrine system, and
'twang' your way to sustainable health!
Paperback: 978-1-84694-503-8 ebook: 978-1-78099-697-4

Readers of ebooks can buy or view any of these bestsellers by clicking on the live link in the title. Most titles are published in paperback and as an ebook. Paperbacks are available in traditional bookshops. Both print and ebook formats are available online.

Find more titles and sign up to our readers' newsletter at http://www.johnhuntpublishing.com/mind-body-spirit

Follow us on Facebook at https://www.facebook.com/OBooks/ and Twitter at https://twitter.com/obooks

Printed and bound by PG in the USA